The Money Habits Book

Crafted by Skriuwer

Copyright © 2024 by Skriuwer.

All rights reserved. No part of this book may be used or reproduced in any form whatsoever without written permission except in the case of brief quotations in critical articles or reviews.

For more information, contact : **kontakt@skriuwer.com** (www.skriuwer.com)

TABLE OF CONTENTS

CHAPTER 1: INTRODUCTION TO A POSITIVE MONEY MINDSET

- Why mindset shapes financial outcomes
- Identifying and replacing negative beliefs
- Building small actions that lead to long-term change

CHAPTER 2: SETTING A CLEAR VISION FOR FINANCIAL SUCCESS

- Defining short-term, medium-term, and long-term goals
- Turning dreams into measurable targets
- Staying motivated through clarity and purpose

CHAPTER 3: BUILDING CONSISTENT SAVING HABITS

- Starting small and automating your savings
- Overcoming barriers to saving regularly
- Tracking progress and celebrating milestones

CHAPTER 4: UNDERSTANDING AND CREATING EFFECTIVE BUDGETS

- Essential budget categories (needs, wants, savings)
- Choosing a budgeting method (envelope system, 50/30/20, etc.)
- Reviewing and adjusting as life changes

CHAPTER 5: MANAGING AND REDUCING DEBT

- *Strategizing debt payoff (snowball or avalanche)*
- *Negotiating lower rates and avoiding further debt*
- *Building habits that prevent debt recurrence*

CHAPTER 6: BUILDING AN EMERGENCY FUND FOR PEACE OF MIND

- *Why emergency savings are critical*
- *Deciding on the right fund size*
- *Where to keep your emergency money*

CHAPTER 7: BASICS OF INVESTING AND GROWING YOUR MONEY

- *Risk vs. return and the importance of diversification*
- *Stocks, bonds, and funds explained*
- *Setting investment goals and timelines*

CHAPTER 8: THE POWER OF COMPOUND INTEREST

- *How compound interest accelerates wealth*
- *Time horizon and reinvestment strategies*
- *Leveraging compounding in everyday finance*

CHAPTER 9: DEFINING AND TRACKING FINANCIAL GOALS

- *SMART goal setting for clearer targets*
- *Breaking large ambitions into smaller steps*
- *Staying motivated with milestones and progress checks*

CHAPTER 10: SMART SPENDING AND FRUGAL LIVING

- *Needs vs. wants and mindful purchasing*
- *Strategic shopping, meal planning, and negotiation*
- *Balancing enjoyment with wise financial choices*

CHAPTER 11: INCREASING YOUR INCOME WITH SIDE HUSTLES AND MORE

- *Identifying marketable skills and opportunities*
- *Balancing extra work with your main job and life*
- *Pricing, negotiation, and scaling side ventures*

CHAPTER 12: THE IMPORTANCE OF PERSISTENCE AND DISCIPLINE

- *Staying consistent with financial routines*
- *Handling setbacks and maintaining motivation*
- *Long-term gains through disciplined choices*

CHAPTER 13: MASTERING NEGOTIATION AND GETTING GOOD DEALS

- *Preparation and polite assertiveness in bargaining*
- *Negotiating big purchases, salaries, and everyday bills*
- *Knowing when to walk away or explore creative solutions*

CHAPTER 14: PLANNING FOR RETIREMENT AND LONG-TERM SECURITY

- *Using tax-advantaged accounts (401(k), IRAs, etc.)*
- *Assessing how much you need for retirement*
- *Adjusting contributions and allocations over time*

CHAPTER 15: TEACHING MONEY HABITS TO CHILDREN

- *Introducing basic budgeting and saving concepts*
- *Allowances, chores, and linking money to effort*
- *Guiding teens on credit, debt, and future planning*

CHAPTER 16: GIVING, GENEROSITY, AND THE IMPACT ON WEALTH

- *How generosity shapes an abundance mindset*
- *Forms of giving (time, money, skills) and their benefits*
- *Balancing personal goals with community support*

CHAPTER 17: NAVIGATING TAXES AND LEGAL STRUCTURES

- Understanding income tax and other tax types
- Choosing the right business entity (sole proprietor, LLC, etc.)
- Record-keeping and strategies for reducing tax burdens

CHAPTER 18: BALANCING HEALTH AND WEALTH

- The financial cost of neglecting physical and mental well-being
- Preventive care, insurance, and stress management
- Incorporating healthy habits on a budget

CHAPTER 19: AVOIDING COMMON FINANCIAL MISTAKES

- Overspending, credit card pitfalls, and skipping an emergency fund
- Emotional investing, trying to time the market, or ignoring insurance
- Recovering from errors and preventing repeats

CHAPTER 20: YOUR ONGOING JOURNEY TO FINANCIAL FREEDOM

- Adapting goals over time and continuous learning
- Celebrating milestones without becoming complacent
- Aligning finances with values and embracing flexibility

CHAPTER 1: INTRODUCTION TO A POSITIVE MONEY MINDSET

1.1 Why Mindset Matters

Let us begin by talking about your thoughts. The way we think can change our whole lives. When we talk about money, many people have fears or worries. They might say, "I will never have enough money," or "I am just bad with money," and so on. These thoughts can stop us from moving forward. On the other hand, having a positive mindset means believing that we can do well. It means being open to learning about money. It means expecting that we can grow our wealth and have financial success if we follow the right steps.

A positive mindset is not magic. It does not mean money will fall from the sky just because we think happy thoughts. Instead, a positive mindset makes us more likely to do certain things. For example, when we believe we can succeed with money, we are more open to learning new tips. We are more patient with ourselves, and we keep trying even if we make mistakes. This belief changes our actions, and our actions change our results.

1.2 Common Negative Beliefs About Money

Many of us grow up hearing negative things about money. We might hear that "money is the root of all problems" or that "only greedy people want to be rich." Some of us learn to think that if we want more money, it means we love money more than people. In other cases, we might think we are not "smart enough" or "good enough" to handle money properly.

These beliefs can become big barriers. They make us afraid to take risks or to learn. We might think, "If I become successful, then I am a bad person." But that is not true. Money itself is a tool. What we do with money is what matters. If we use money to help ourselves, our families, and the people around us, it can be a positive force. If we do not use it well, it can cause trouble. But the tool itself is neutral.

1.3 Replacing Negative Beliefs

To change negative beliefs, you first have to know you have them. A good way to start is to write down all the thoughts that come to mind when you think about money. Maybe your list includes, "I never have enough," or "I am bad at saving," or "Money is too complicated." Next, look at each belief and ask, "Is this really true?" or "Where did I learn this?" You might find you believe something because someone told you when you were young, not because you tested it yourself.

Once you see that these negative beliefs are not always true, you can replace them with better ones. For example, instead of saying, "I can never be good with money," you can say, "I am learning about money every day." Or, "I have made mistakes, but I am improving." This shift in language seems small, but it makes a big difference in how you feel and act.

1.4 The Power of Small Actions

A positive mindset leads to small actions that grow into big results. When you tell yourself, "I can learn," you might start reading a few pages of a money book each day. You might decide to save just a tiny amount of money each week. Over time, these small steps add up. Think of it like planting seeds in a garden. Each seed is small, but with water, sunlight, and care, it turns into a plant that can feed you for a long time.

At first, small steps may not look like much. But a positive mindset helps you stay consistent. Instead of giving up after a week, you keep going. Soon, you may find yourself with a growing savings account or a new source of income. The best part is, these good habits tend to build on each other. When you see success in one area—like saving money—you feel more confident to try new things, like investing or starting a side business.

1.5 Examples of a Healthy Money Mindset

Here are some examples of what a healthy money mindset looks like in everyday thoughts:

1. "I am capable of learning about money."
2. "Mistakes are not failures. They are lessons."
3. "I respect money as a helpful tool."

4. "I believe I can earn more by increasing my knowledge or skills."
5. "Saving money is good for my future."

These might sound simple, but thinking this way can change the path of your life. By keeping these thoughts in mind, you treat money decisions with care. You also treat yourself with kindness. You stop saying, "I am not good enough," and start saying, "I can get better."

1.6 Facing Challenges with a Positive Mindset

Life will always have challenges. You might lose a job, face medical bills, or deal with other surprises. A positive mindset does not mean these things will never happen. It means that when they do happen, you believe you can find a way through. When you face a money challenge, you stop and ask, "What can I learn from this?" Then you look for answers.

Some people, when they face a big bill they cannot pay, freeze up or ignore it. Others say, "Okay, this is hard, but maybe I can work out a payment plan or get an extra job for a while." The second approach is healthier. It might still be difficult, but it usually leads to solutions. The first approach might lead to more debt or damage to your credit score. A positive mindset helps you see options instead of just problems.

1.7 The Link Between Mindset and Habits

Habits are daily actions we do without much thought. They form from repeated behaviors over time. For example, if you always pick up a cup of coffee in the morning, that is a habit. If you place money into a savings account each month, that is also a habit. Your mindset either makes these habits easier or harder.

If your mindset says, "Saving is a waste of time," then you will not make a habit of saving. On the other hand, if you say, "Saving a little each month helps me reach my goals," you are more likely to save. Over time, it will become something you do naturally, like brushing your teeth. That is how mindset and habits work together.

1.8 Practical Steps to Build a Positive Money Mindset

Let us go through some actions you can take right now:

1. **Daily Affirmations**: Each morning, say something positive about money out loud. For instance, "I can handle money wisely," or "I am improving my money skills every day."
2. **Write Down Goals**: Seeing your goals in writing can train your brain to focus on them. Write financial goals like "I will save $500 in the next three months."
3. **Reflect on Wins**: At the end of each day, think about any positive money move you made. Did you skip an unnecessary purchase? Did you learn a new money tip? Celebrate these small wins.
4. **Surround Yourself with Helpful Resources**: This can be people, books, or videos that talk about money in a positive and educational way. The more you hear that money can be managed, the more you believe it.
5. **Talk About Money in a Good Way**: If you have friends or family who are always negative about money, their mood can rub off on you. Try to speak about money in a calmer, more solution-focused way. This sets the tone for your mindset.

1.9 Mindset Helps You Take Responsibility

Having a strong mindset also means accepting responsibility. We cannot control everything, but we can control our reactions. If you lose money on a bad investment, you could blame the market or blame bad luck. A healthier approach is to look at what you might have missed. Did you fail to research properly? Did you invest money you could not afford to lose? By finding your part in the situation, you learn and grow.

When you take responsibility, you gain power. If everything is someone else's fault, you have no control. But if you find ways you could have done better, then you can change. You can make better decisions next time. This is why a positive mindset is so important: it helps you stay open to learning.

1.10 Changing Your Story

Many of us have old stories about money that we keep telling ourselves. Maybe it is "I am always broke," or "I come from a poor family; I can never change that." It is possible that these stories were true at some point. But do they have to stay true? If you decide to learn, to work on your money habits, and to build new skills, your story can become something else. You can start saying, "I am working on a stable future," or "I am gaining the skills I need to grow."

Changing your story takes time. But it starts with the decision to do so. The chapters ahead will give you practical tips and steps to create new money habits. Keep this positive mindset and remind yourself that you are on a learning path. Every lesson you pick up will help you shape a brighter future.

1.11 Key Takeaways from Chapter 1

1. **Mindset is the Foundation**: Your thoughts set the stage for your money habits.
2. **Replace Negative Beliefs**: Catch negative beliefs and replace them with healthier ones.
3. **Take Small Steps**: Tiny actions each day add up to big changes over time.
4. **Stay Open to Learning**: Mistakes are lessons, not final defeats.
5. **Write Goals and Celebrate Wins**: This keeps you focused and motivated.

1.12 Conclusion

A positive money mindset is like building a strong base for a house. Without it, even the best tools and materials might fall apart. With it, you have the support you need to grow. In the next chapters, we will explore specific habits and methods for handling money well. Keep reminding yourself that you can learn and do better. This mindset will help you each step of the way.

CHAPTER 2: SETTING A CLEAR VISION FOR FINANCIAL SUCCESS

2.1 The Importance of Having a Financial Vision

Now that we have looked at how mindset plays a major role in our money habits, it is time to focus on **vision**. Your vision is a clear picture of where you want to go. It is like a map for your future. If you do not have a map, you might travel in circles or get stuck. A financial vision tells you what success looks like and how you might get there.

Many people do not take time to form a vision for their financial lives. They might have vague wishes like "I want more money," but they never define what "more money" really means. Having a specific vision pushes you to be clear. Do you want to buy a home? Do you want to retire by age 60? Do you want to start a charity? A well-defined vision helps you set goals that match your true desires.

2.2 Imagining Your Ideal Future

Before we talk about setting goals or making plans, it helps to imagine your dream future. Take a moment to think about your life five or ten years from now. Picture where you live, what kind of work you do, how you spend your days. Do you see yourself working for a company you love, or running your own business, or perhaps teaching others? How do you spend your free time? Are you traveling the world or staying close to home?

These details paint a picture of what you value. When you think carefully about your future, you start to see what financial success means to you personally. Maybe your main dream is to have the freedom to spend time with your kids. Maybe you want a comfortable home in a quiet neighborhood. Whatever it is, hold that picture in your mind. This vision will guide you as you make money decisions.

2.3 Turning Your Vision into Measurable Goals

Once you have a vision of your future, you need to translate it into goals that you can measure. For example, if your dream is to buy a house, you might set a goal of saving a 20% down payment within five years. If your dream is to travel, you might set a goal of saving a certain amount of money each year for trips. The more specific, the better.

Here is a simple process:

1. **Write Down Your Vision**: Put your dream future on paper.
2. **Pick Out Specific Desires**: List the key elements (like "own a home," "travel yearly," "pay off student loans").
3. **Set Clear Targets**: For each desire, define how much money you might need and by when.
4. **Break Them Down**: If you need $20,000 for a down payment in five years, that is $4,000 a year. Divide that further into $333 per month.

This breakdown helps you see exactly how to work toward your goals each day. It turns big dreams into small actions. You know that if you can save $333 per month, you will stay on track. If you cannot manage $333, maybe you can do $200. The point is to start somewhere and keep going.

2.4 Finding Motivation in Your Vision

It is easy to say you want a certain amount of money, but if you do not feel excited about the reason behind it, you might quit when things get tough. This is where a strong vision comes in. When you have a clear mental picture of how your life will look, that becomes your "why." It is the reason you keep going.

Maybe you want to save money so you can send your child to a good school. Maybe you want to open a small café because you love cooking and want to share your creations. When you connect your goals to something you deeply care about, you are more likely to stick with them. You will wake up each day and think, "This action leads me closer to my dream."

2.5 Balancing Short-Term and Long-Term Visions

It can be tempting to focus only on long-term goals, like retirement or buying a dream home. But do not forget about the short term. If you set all your goals for 20 years from now, you might lose motivation. That is why it is good to have both short-term and long-term targets.

Short-term goals could be things you want to achieve in the next year. For example, building a mini emergency fund of $1,000, or paying off a small credit card debt. Long-term goals might be saving for a house or retiring at a certain age. Having a mix of both keeps you moving forward, while also letting you see progress soon.

2.6 Overcoming Obstacles to Your Vision

Even the best vision can run into real-life roadblocks. You might face health issues, lose a job, or have family emergencies. Do not let these challenges erase your dream. Instead, think of them as detours. You might need to slow down or adjust your goals, but you do not have to abandon them.

When you hit a barrier, sit down and revisit your vision. Ask yourself, "Which parts of my plan are still possible right now?" Maybe you need to save a smaller amount each month. Or perhaps you need to push your timeline back a bit. The important thing is to keep some form of momentum. If you cannot run, walk. If you cannot walk, crawl. But do not stop.

2.7 Tracking Your Progress

To keep your vision alive, track your progress regularly. This can be done in a notebook, a spreadsheet, or an app. Write down your goals, the deadline, and the actions you plan to take. Each week or month, update where you stand. How much did you save? Did you invest any money? Did you lower your debt?

This tracking serves two purposes. First, it helps you see if you are on course. If you are behind, you can fix your actions. If you are ahead, you can pat yourself on the back. Second, it builds excitement. Seeing your own progress can be incredibly motivating.

2.8 Surrounding Yourself with Support

A vision becomes easier to achieve when you have the right people around you. If your friends and family are supportive of your goals, you will find it easier to stay on track. On the other hand, if they constantly doubt you or belittle your dreams, it can be tough. You might need to limit the time you spend talking about your goals with negative people.

In some cases, you can find support groups or online communities. Many people share the same goals, like saving for a house or paying off debt. By connecting with them, you can learn tips, share your experiences, and stay inspired. The key is to have at least one person who believes in your vision and can cheer you on or offer advice when you are stuck.

2.9 Adjusting Your Vision Over Time

Your life might change in unexpected ways. Maybe you discover a new passion, or your family grows. It is normal for your vision to shift. Setting a vision does not mean you are stuck with it forever. It is like a living document that changes as you learn and grow.

For example, you might decide that you no longer want to buy a large house but would rather travel frequently. That is okay. What matters is that you always have a plan to work on, even if the plan evolves. Keep checking your vision at least once a year. Ask yourself if it still matches what you want out of life. If not, change it.

2.10 Breaking Down Bigger Visions

Sometimes, a vision can feel too big. Let us say you dream of becoming financially free by age 50, but you are already 40 and have a lot of debt. That might seem impossible. The key is to break the big vision into smaller pieces:

1. **Pay Off High-Interest Debt**: Focus on credit cards or high-interest loans first.
2. **Build an Emergency Fund**: Have at least a few months of expenses saved.
3. **Start Investing**: Even small amounts in a retirement account can grow significantly over a decade.
4. **Look for Ways to Earn More**: Could you change jobs, pick up freelance work, or invest in a small venture?

By splitting your huge goal into bite-sized tasks, you get a roadmap. Each step completed is progress toward the final picture.

2.11 Celebrating Milestones

When you reach a goal, take time to celebrate. If you managed to save your first $1,000 emergency fund, reward yourself in a modest way. This does not mean spending half of it on a party. It could be as simple as a favorite meal at home or a day off to relax. Celebrations mark your achievements and keep you excited for the next milestone.

Just be careful not to overspend on celebrations. The point is to acknowledge your hard work, not to set yourself back financially. Sometimes, a heartfelt note in your journal or a small treat can do wonders for your motivation.

2.12 Vision and Daily Habits

Having a vision means nothing if you do not act on it each day. One of the best ways to keep your vision alive is to turn it into daily habits. For example, if your vision involves writing a book that will eventually make you money, then writing for 30 minutes each day becomes a habit. If your vision involves being debt-free, then checking your expenses weekly and paying extra toward your debt becomes a habit.

By pairing daily habits with your larger vision, you make progress even if you do not see results right away. Over time, these habits become automatic, and your vision starts to become reality.

2.13 The Emotional Side of Vision

We often forget that money is emotional. We feel stressed, proud, scared, or excited about it. A strong vision taps into these feelings in a good way. You might keep a photo of a place you want to visit on your wall. Each time you see it, you remember why you are skipping unnecessary purchases. You remember why you are trying to earn more. This emotional connection keeps you going.

If you find yourself losing interest in your goals, it might be because your vision is no longer inspiring you. Revisit your dream and see if it still brings a spark of excitement. If not, adjust it. Life is too short to chase a vision you no longer care about.

2.14 Making Your Vision Real

It is common to have big dreams but no plan. A dream without a plan can stay just that—a dream. To make your vision real, you have to put it into steps and start taking action. For instance, if your vision is to start a small business, your steps might include:

1. Research similar businesses.
2. Write a simple business plan.
3. Save some money or find investors to start.
4. Test your idea on a small scale.
5. Officially launch your business.

Each step might take weeks or months, but as long as you are moving forward, you are turning your vision into reality.

2.15 Staying Flexible

While it is good to be focused, it is also good to stay flexible. Sometimes, a goal will not go as planned. Maybe you wanted to buy a house in a certain neighborhood but found the prices were out of your range. Could you look in a nearby area? Could you rent first while you save more? Flexibility means you keep your main vision in mind—owning a home—but you stay open to different ways of reaching it.

2.16 Vision Supports a Positive Mindset

In Chapter 1, we learned about having a positive money mindset. A clear vision strengthens that mindset. When you can picture a better future, you are less likely to feel hopeless. You see that the steps you take every day—like saving money or saying no to unnecessary purchases—are building toward something you truly want. This feeling can give you the energy to keep going when things get tough.

2.17 Helping Others See Your Vision

Sometimes, you have family or close friends who do not understand why you are changing your money habits. They might tease you for saving too much or question why you will not go out to fancy dinners anymore. One way to handle this is by gently explaining your vision. You can say something like, "I am working on saving for a down payment on a house. That is why I am cutting back on some expenses. It really matters to me."

If they care about you, they may try to understand and support you once they see the bigger picture. If they still do not understand, you might need to limit how much you share, so you do not get discouraged.

2.18 Revisiting Your Vision in Tough Times

When things do not go as planned, it is tempting to give up. Maybe you wanted to pay off your credit card debt by the end of the year, but unexpected medical bills set you back. In these moments, go back to your vision. Why did you want to be free of debt in the first place? How will it change your life once you are free from that burden?

By focusing on the original "why," you rekindle your motivation. You remember that your actions have a purpose. Yes, the timeline might shift, but the goal still stands. This perspective keeps you from throwing in the towel just because things got hard.

2.19 Finding Role Models

Look for people who have already done what you want to do. If your vision is to retire early, search for stories of people who achieved early retirement. If you want to start a successful side business, read about those who have done it. These role models can show you that your vision is possible. They can also provide tips or strategies you had not considered.

Even if you do not know them personally, their stories can inspire you. You might learn about how they saved 50% of their income or how they invested in simple index funds to grow their money. It proves that an ordinary person, not just lottery winners or celebrities, can make big changes.

2.20 Conclusion and Next Steps

Creating a clear vision for financial success is a key step in your money journey. This vision should be personal to you. It should reflect what you value in life. When you know what you want, you can break it down into goals, track your progress, and stay motivated even when challenges arise.

In the next chapters, you will learn practical ways to build a strong foundation—like saving consistently and making budgets that work. Remember, each action you take is a building block for the future you want. Keep your vision bright in your mind, and let it guide your daily decisions. You have the power to shape your financial destiny, one step at a time.

CHAPTER 3: BUILDING CONSISTENT SAVING HABITS

3.1 Why Saving Matters

Saving money is one of the most important habits you can develop. It is the foundation for many of your financial goals—whether it is buying a house, paying for education, taking a dream vacation, or simply having peace of mind. When you save, you are setting aside money for a future need or want. This act alone can protect you from financial stress and help you achieve stability. It can also give you the freedom to make big decisions in life, like changing jobs or starting a business, without the same level of worry about money.

Yet, many people skip saving because they think they do not earn enough. Others see saving as boring or too hard. They may feel that their money disappears too quickly to set anything aside. But saving does not have to be complicated. Consistent saving habits can be formed by small actions repeated over time. When you practice saving often, it becomes second nature.

3.2 Overcoming Barriers to Saving

Before we talk about *how* to save, let us deal with the barriers that may prevent you from saving regularly.

1. **Feeling You Do Not Earn Enough**: You might believe your paycheck is too small to allow any savings. While it is true that lower income makes saving more challenging, it does not make it impossible. Even setting aside a tiny amount each week or each month can add up over time.
2. **Lack of Motivation**: If saving feels like a chore, you might avoid it. This is why connecting saving to a personal goal (like a new car or a dream trip) can help. When you see how saving leads you to something you really want, it becomes more motivating.
3. **Temptations**: Advertisements, social media, and peer pressure can make you want to spend more than you earn. Resisting these temptations requires discipline and a focus on long-term benefits instead of short-term pleasures.

4. **Unclear Goals**: When you do not know why you are saving, it is easy to forget to save. If you have a clear picture of what you want to do with your saved money—such as a home down payment or an emergency fund—it is easier to take saving seriously.
5. **Immediate Needs**: Sometimes, your expenses really do outweigh your income, especially if you have unexpected medical bills or family obligations. In those times, saving may need to be small or temporarily paused, but the key is not to give up entirely. Even saving a dollar a day, if possible, keeps the habit alive.

3.3 Starting Small

A common mistake is to think you have to save large chunks of money right away. This can be discouraging and lead you to quit if you cannot keep up. Instead, start with an amount you can handle without feeling overly strained. For some, that might be $10 a week, for others $100, or even $1. The actual amount matters less than the habit itself.

Think of saving like exercise. Doing 10 push-ups every day is better than doing 50 once a week and then stopping completely. Consistency is key. If you save even a small amount regularly, you build a strong financial habit. Over time, you can increase the amount as your income grows or your expenses go down.

3.4 Automating Your Savings

One of the best ways to ensure you save consistently is to automate it. Many banks and employers offer services that let you transfer a fixed amount of money from your checking account or paycheck into a savings account. This can happen on payday or once a month, depending on your preference. Because it is automatic, you do not have to rely on willpower each time. The money leaves your account before you get the chance to spend it.

Automation also removes the temptation to skip saving "just this once." By making the process automatic, you prioritize your savings goals. Over time, you may not even miss the money because you adjust your lifestyle around what is left in your checking account.

3.5 Different Types of Savings

Not all savings accounts are the same, and not all savings goals are the same. Here are a few types:

1. **Emergency Fund**: This is your safety net for unexpected costs, like medical bills or car repairs. Many experts recommend saving at least three to six months' worth of living expenses.
2. **Short-Term Savings**: This could be for a vacation, a new computer, or any purchase you plan to make within the next year or two. Keeping short-term savings in a separate account helps you avoid mixing it with daily spending money.
3. **Long-Term Savings**: This includes saving for a down payment on a house, for college tuition, or for a big goal that might take several years. You might choose a higher-interest savings account or another secure option to help the money grow a bit more.
4. **Retirement Savings**: While we will discuss retirement in a later chapter in more detail, it is important to note that retirement savings is another form of long-term savings. It often sits in specialized accounts that can only be accessed later in life without penalties.

By splitting your savings into different "buckets" or accounts, you make it easier to see how much progress you are making toward specific goals. It also prevents you from dipping into emergency funds for non-urgent wants.

3.6 Strategies to Boost Your Saving

There are many ways to increase the amount you save over time. Here are some ideas:

1. **Save Your Windfalls**: If you receive a bonus at work, a tax refund, or a birthday gift in cash, consider putting a big portion (or all) of it into savings right away. This is money you did not expect in your normal budget, so it is easier to save without missing it.
2. **Pay Yourself First**: Many people wait until the end of the month to see if anything is left to save. A better approach is to treat saving like a bill you must pay before other expenses. Once you get your paycheck, move a set amount to savings. Then learn to live on what remains.

3. **Cut Back on Small Costs**: Look for areas where small, regular expenses add up, such as daily coffee runs or eating out for lunch every day. You do not have to cut them all out, but reducing them can free up cash for savings.
   4. **Set Clear Targets**: For example, decide you want to have $1,000 in your emergency fund by a certain date. Having a clear target amount and deadline pushes you to find ways to reach it faster.
   5. **Reward Yourself**: Saving can feel dull if there is never any reward. Consider small, sensible treats when you hit a milestone. It might be a nice meal at home or a day trip somewhere local. This way, saving feels like a journey with milestones, not just a sacrifice.

3.7 The Emotional Side of Saving

Money is not just about numbers; it also ties into our emotions. We may feel secure, anxious, proud, or fearful about our financial situation. Building a saving habit can improve our sense of security. When you see your account balance growing, you may feel calmer about your future. This emotional reward can be powerful and can motivate you to keep saving.

On the other hand, if you are used to impulse buying or get a thrill from big purchases, you might feel bored or sad at first when you choose to save instead of spend. A good way to handle this is to find a balance. Save as much as you can, but also allow for a small portion of your income for guilt-free spending. This keeps you from feeling deprived.

3.8 Common Pitfalls in Saving

While building a saving habit, watch out for these common mistakes:

   1. **Dipping into Savings for Non-Essentials**: It can be tempting to "borrow" from your savings for a quick trip or a new gadget. Doing this often can destroy your progress. If you need fun money, plan for it in your regular budget, not from your savings.
   2. **Not Having a Goal**: If you do not know what you are saving for, you are more likely to lose motivation. Tie each chunk of savings to a clear purpose or goal.
   3. **Keeping Savings in Hard-to-Access Places**: While it can be helpful to have money in an account that is separate from your daily checking, it

should not be so inaccessible that you cannot reach it in a true emergency. For example, a high-yield online savings account is fine, but if it takes weeks to access the funds, that might be an issue in a real crisis.
4. **Ignoring Inflation or Interest Rates**: If you keep large amounts of money in a place that has zero interest, inflation will reduce its value over time. While we will explore investing in later chapters, it is important to at least choose a savings account that pays some interest, if possible, especially for longer-term goals.

3.9 Making Saving a Lifestyle

When saving becomes part of your lifestyle, it stops feeling like a chore. For instance, you might start finding enjoyment in cooking at home rather than eating out, and put the extra money into savings. You might look forward to seeing your account balance climb every month. This lifestyle shift is what makes saving sustainable over the long term.

You can also share your progress with supportive friends or family members (if you feel comfortable). Celebrating your small wins with others can add extra motivation and accountability. In time, you will likely find that focusing on savings becomes second nature, and you might wonder how you ever lived without this habit.

3.10 Tracking and Reviewing

Once you start saving, do not forget to track your progress regularly. This could be done once a month or once a week, depending on your preference. Write down the balance in each savings account and see how it has changed since the last check. If you are not making the progress you hoped for, look at your spending or your income sources to see if adjustments are needed.

A monthly or quarterly review is also a good time to make sure your goals are still relevant. Maybe your situation changed, and you need to shift priorities. As long as you keep an eye on things, you can make those changes smoothly.

3.11 Real-Life Examples of Saving Success

Let us look at a couple of short examples (without repeating previous points) to see how saving habits can really help people:

1. **Brian's Story**: Brian was living paycheck to paycheck and had no savings. He decided to open a simple savings account at his bank and automate $50 a week to go into that account. At first, it seemed small, but after six months, he had $1,200. This was enough to cover an unexpected car repair without using his credit card. Now, he has increased his weekly savings to $75 because he saw how helpful that emergency fund can be.
2. **Sara's Story**: Sara set a goal to buy new furniture for her living room. She did not want to rely on a credit card. So she figured out she needed $2,000. She gave herself 10 months, which meant saving $200 a month. She cut down on dining out and made coffee at home. Each month, she put $200 into a separate "new furniture" account. By the end of the 10 months, she bought the furniture without going into debt—and she felt proud.

These examples show that you do not need massive amounts of money to get started. You just need to be consistent. Over time, small amounts grow. Seeing tangible results is a huge confidence booster.

3.12 Turning Saving into a Habit

Let us go step by step to form a saving habit:

1. **Identify Why You Are Saving**: Write down your goals—emergency fund, home, vacation, etc.
2. **Choose an Amount**: Pick a sum you can reasonably manage. Even if it is $10 a month, start there.
3. **Decide Where to Save**: Open a dedicated savings account. Look for one that pays a bit of interest if possible.
4. **Automate**: Set up an automatic transfer from your checking to your savings.
5. **Check In**: Mark your calendar to review your savings balance monthly.

Follow these steps, and adjust as needed. If money gets tight, lower the amount but keep the habit going. If you get a raise, bump up the amount. The key is consistency over time.

3.13 Dealing with Setbacks

Life can throw curveballs. You might have to dip into your emergency fund because of a medical bill or job loss. When that happens, do not beat yourself up. That is exactly why the fund exists. Use it if you must, but once you are back on your feet, rebuild it as soon as you can.

If you find yourself feeling discouraged, remember that even having some savings is better than none. Instead of giving up, think of how much harder it would be if you had not saved anything at all. Each setback is a chance to learn what you can do differently next time, whether that means adjusting your budget or aiming for an even larger emergency fund.

3.14 The Bigger Picture

While saving itself is crucial, it is also just one part of a bigger financial picture. You will learn about budgeting, investing, paying off debt, and more in the chapters ahead. Think of saving as the safe, steady part of your overall strategy. With a healthy cushion in place, you will feel more confident taking on other financial projects, like investing in the stock market or starting a side business. That cushion acts as your safety net, letting you move forward with less fear of unexpected setbacks.

3.15 Inspiring Others to Save

Sometimes, your family or friends might not understand why you are turning down certain activities or purchases to save money. You might face pressure to keep spending. In such situations, explain the benefits you have seen: less stress, more confidence in handling emergencies, and the progress you have made toward specific goals. Your example can inspire them. You do not have to push or lecture—just let your success speak for itself. If they see you are happy and secure, they might start asking questions about how to do the same.

3.16 Stay Patient and Keep Going

Saving is not a get-rich-quick scheme. It is a steady process that rewards patience. You might look at your balance one day and feel disappointed that it is not larger. But remember, every dollar saved is a step forward. Patience means understanding that real change takes time. The more consistent you are, the faster you will see progress, even if it feels slow at first.

Try to avoid comparing your savings with others. Everyone has different incomes, responsibilities, and life circumstances. The key is to focus on your own goals and what you can do. The more you put in, the more you get out—both in terms of account balance and peace of mind.

3.17 Chapter Summary

- **Saving is Essential**: It protects you from unexpected financial problems and helps you reach your dreams.
- **Start with Small Steps**: Every little bit counts. Form the habit, then build on it.
- **Automate**: Use automatic transfers to remove the need for willpower every time.
- **Track and Celebrate**: See your progress and reward yourself at milestones.
- **Stay Adaptable**: Life changes, so adjust your saving goals and amounts as needed.

3.18 Conclusion

Saving is about building a future you can rely on. By taking consistent steps—no matter how small—you create a cushion that can protect you from emergencies and open doors to new opportunities. Over time, your saving habit becomes a key part of who you are: a person who is proactive, prepared, and hopeful about what lies ahead.

CHAPTER 4: UNDERSTANDING AND CREATING EFFECTIVE BUDGETS

4.1 The Purpose of a Budget

A budget is a plan for how you will use your money over a certain period, usually a month. Many people hear the word "budget" and think of something boring or restrictive. However, a budget does not have to be a punishment. Instead, it is a tool that helps you make sure your income covers your needs and allows for savings and investments. It also helps you avoid overspending and going into unnecessary debt.

Think of a budget as a map. When you want to reach a certain destination financially, your budget shows you which road to take. Without it, you might take random turns (random spending) and never get where you want to go.

4.2 Common Misconceptions About Budgets

There are many misconceptions that keep people from creating or following a budget:

1. **"A Budget Is Only for Rich People"**: This is not true. Budgets are helpful for people at all income levels. Even if you earn a small salary, having a clear plan can reduce stress and help you find small ways to save.
2. **"A Budget Means No Fun"**: Another myth. A good budget includes room for enjoyment, whether that is a small entertainment fund or the occasional treat. It just ensures that you do not overdo it.
3. **"I Can Keep It All in My Head"**: While some people think they can remember all their expenses, surprises usually pop up. Writing a budget down or using a budgeting app makes it harder to forget or ignore any spending categories.
4. **"I Make Enough Money; I Don't Need a Budget"**: Even if you have a high income, without a plan you could still waste money or fail to reach your bigger goals. Budgets give you control, not just security.

4.3 The Basic Steps to Create a Budget

To build an effective budget, follow these steps:

1. **Calculate Your Net Income**: Net income is what you take home after taxes and other deductions. This is the actual amount of money you have to spend or save each month.
2. **List Your Expenses**: Write down or type out all the expenses you can think of—rent, groceries, utilities, transportation, insurance, debt payments, entertainment, subscriptions, and so on. Look at your bank statements and receipts to be sure you are not missing anything.
3. **Categorize Your Spending**: Group your expenses into categories like "Housing," "Food," "Transportation," "Utilities," "Insurance," "Debt Repayment," "Savings," "Fun," etc. This helps you see where your money goes.
4. **Assign Amounts to Each Category**: Decide how much you will spend in each category. Some amounts, like rent, might be fixed. Others, like groceries, can vary each month. Try to assign realistic numbers based on past spending, but also see if there is room to cut back in certain areas.
5. **Track Your Actual Spending**: As the month goes on, keep a record of how much you are actually spending. Compare it to the amounts you set in your budget. If you see that you are overspending in one category, try to adjust.
6. **Adjust and Refine**: Rarely do people get their budget exactly right the first time. You might need a few months to find the right balance. That is normal. Keep adjusting until you have a plan that works for you.

4.4 Different Budgeting Methods

Several budgeting methods exist. The key is to choose one that feels comfortable and easy for you to maintain:

1. **The 50/30/20 Rule**: This simple method divides your monthly net income into three parts:
    - 50% for needs (rent, food, utilities)
    - 30% for wants (entertainment, dining out)
    - 20% for savings or debt repayment
2. This rule is easy to remember, but the percentages may need to be adjusted based on your personal situation.

3. **Zero-Based Budgeting**: Here, you assign a role to every dollar of your income until it "zeros out." For example, if you earn $3,000 a month, you will allocate exactly $3,000 among your various categories, including savings. This method ensures that you know exactly where each dollar goes.
4. **Envelope System**: Traditionally done with physical envelopes, each envelope is labeled with a spending category—like groceries, gas, entertainment—and filled with the cash you plan to use for that category for the month. Once the envelope is empty, you cannot spend more on that category. Digital versions of this system also exist now.
5. **App-Based Budgeting**: Some people prefer a budgeting app that automatically tracks expenses and categorizes them. This approach can save time, but you should still review your spending to make sure the app is grouping things correctly.

Each method has its pros and cons. The best one is the one you can stick with. You might try one method for a month or two and then switch if it is not working well for you.

4.5 Balancing Needs, Wants, and Savings

A big part of budgeting is learning how to balance your needs (things you must pay for to live, like rent and food), your wants (extras that make life enjoyable, like a hobby or eating out), and your savings (money set aside for future goals or emergencies). If you focus only on needs and savings and never allow any wants, you might feel deprived and give up. On the other hand, if you spend too much on wants, you may not have enough left for savings.

A balanced budget often follows a formula, but it can be personal. Some people might choose to keep wants very low for a short period if they want to aggressively pay down debt or build savings. Others might spread their money more evenly across all categories. The key is making sure that your choices match your priorities and long-term goals.

4.6 Budgeting with Irregular Income

Not everyone has a fixed monthly paycheck. If you are a freelancer, seasonal worker, or have a job based on tips or commissions, your income might change from month to month. Budgeting becomes trickier, but still possible.

1. **Calculate an Average**: Look at your earnings from the past several months to estimate a conservative monthly average.
2. **Set Up a "Variable Income" Fund**: Try to have a small buffer in your checking account. In months you earn more, put extra into that buffer. In months you earn less, use some of that buffer to cover expenses.
3. **Focus on Essentials First**: Make sure your main bills are covered. The rest of your spending should be flexible, depending on your actual income each month.

4.7 Handling Unexpected Expenses

Even the best budget can be disrupted by an unexpected expense, like a sudden medical bill or a broken appliance. This is why having an emergency fund is crucial. Still, it helps to have a category in your monthly budget for miscellaneous or "unexpected" expenses. If nothing unexpected happens that month, you can roll that amount into savings or pay extra on debt.

4.8 Reviewing and Tweaking Your Budget

Your budget is not a "set it and forget it" tool. Each month can bring new changes—maybe you find a cheaper phone plan, or your rent goes up. Make it a habit to review your budget at least once a month to see how well it is working. Ask yourself questions like:

- Did I overspend in certain categories? Why?
- Did I underspend in any category? Can I redirect those savings?
- Are my income or expenses about to change?
- Are there any subscriptions or bills I can negotiate or cancel?

Based on the answers, adjust your budget for the next month. Over time, you will refine it so that it feels more natural and helps you reach your goals consistently.

4.9 Tools and Resources

There are many tools to help you budget, from pen-and-paper approaches to spreadsheet templates to mobile apps. Here are some general suggestions (not brand names) for the types of tools you might explore:

1. **Spreadsheets**: You can set up columns for income, expenses, and differences. You can also add categories and color-code them.

2. **Budgeting Apps**: These apps link to your bank accounts and credit cards, track your purchases, and show you if you are on track.
3. **Bank Notifications**: Most banks let you set up alerts for low balances or large transactions. These can keep you aware of your spending.
4. **Online Calculators**: Some websites have calculators that help you plan for goals like saving for a down payment or paying off debt.

Pick what fits your comfort level. The best resource is the one you will actually use consistently.

4.10 Dealing with Debt in a Budget

If you have debt—like credit card balances, student loans, or a car payment—your budget should include a plan for paying it off. You might prioritize high-interest debt first, or follow a method where you pay off the smallest balances first for motivation. Either way, treat debt repayment as a necessary category in your monthly plan. That way, you will steadily work toward becoming debt-free.

While it might feel frustrating to allocate a large portion of your budget to debt payments, remember that each payment is an investment in your future freedom. The faster you pay off high-interest debt, the more money you free up for saving and investing later.

4.11 Living Within Your Means

A budget helps you live within your means by showing if your expenses exceed your income. If your total expenses add up to more than what you earn, you have only two choices: lower your expenses or increase your income. While this can sound harsh, being aware of the situation is better than ignoring it and falling deeper into debt.

If you find you have a shortfall, look at your budget categories to see where you can cut back. Can you reduce your grocery bill by meal planning? Can you cancel or pause a subscription you rarely use? You might also explore ways to earn more, such as a side job or selling items you no longer need. Sometimes, small changes in multiple areas can add up to fill that gap.

4.12 Setting Realistic Goals

One reason people fail at budgeting is setting unrealistic targets. Maybe you decide you will only spend $50 on groceries for the whole month, but you actually need $200. If you are too strict, you will blow the budget and feel discouraged. A better approach is to start with your current spending, then see if you can lower it by a reasonable amount.

For instance, if you currently spend $300 a month on groceries, try reducing it to $250. See if you can make that work by shopping sales or planning meals. Gradual changes are more sustainable.

4.13 Budgeting for Fun and Relaxation

It is a mistake to leave out entertainment or leisure from your budget. These are parts of life that can bring joy and maintain your mental health. Even if you are in a tight financial spot, consider leaving a small portion for something you enjoy—like a hobby or a night out with friends once a month. If you completely remove fun from your budget, you may end up feeling deprived and overspending out of frustration later.

4.14 Building a Family Budget

If you live with a partner or family, budgeting becomes a team effort. That means discussing financial goals and setting categories together. If one person is always spending outside the budget, it can create tension. Clear communication is crucial.

- **Family Meetings**: Have monthly family budget meetings where everyone can share updates, concerns, and ideas.
- **Delegate Responsibilities**: Maybe one person handles groceries, while another handles utilities or mortgage payments.
- **Agree on Goals**: Whether it is saving for a family vacation or paying off debt, make sure everyone is on the same page.

By working together, you can often spot more ways to save or earn, and you will reduce arguments about money.

4.15 Adjusting for Life Changes

Your budget might work perfectly for a while, then life changes happen. You might switch jobs, have a child, or face an unexpected medical issue. In these times, do not panic. Simply revisit your budget and adjust your categories and priorities. It might mean cutting back on non-essentials for a period or focusing on building up an emergency fund again.

4.16 The Emotional Side of Budgeting

Budgeting can trigger various emotions. Some feel a sense of relief and control. Others may feel restricted or anxious about seeing their spending laid out in black and white. The best approach is to view a budget as a supportive framework, not a cage. It is there to help you direct your money toward what matters most to you, not to judge you.

If you find budgeting very stressful, start small. Maybe just track your biggest expenses first, like housing, groceries, and transportation. As you get more comfortable, add more details.

4.17 How Budgeting Ties In with Your Vision

Recall in Chapter 2 how we discussed having a clear vision for your financial future. A budget is one of the main tools that helps make that vision real. If your vision is to own a home, your budget can include saving for a down payment. If your vision is to travel, you can budget a monthly contribution to a "travel fund." Each day-to-day budgeting decision links back to the bigger picture, giving those small decisions real meaning.

4.18 Learning from Mistakes

Everyone makes budget mistakes—like forgetting a major expense or spending more than planned on a big sale. These mistakes are normal. The important thing is to learn from them. Ask yourself: "Why did this happen?" and "How can I prevent it next time?" Maybe you need to set a reminder for upcoming yearly bills, or maybe you need to put a limit on impulsive online shopping. Each mistake, when acknowledged, can improve your budgeting process.

4.19 Celebrating Your Budget Wins

When you follow your budget successfully for a month or two, celebrate. Maybe you managed to stay under your grocery limit or paid extra on your credit card. Give yourself a small reward—within reason—that will encourage you to keep going. It could be a homemade dessert, a movie night at home, or something else that feels special but does not break the bank.

Over time, these small celebrations can keep the process fun and engaging. They also give you something to look forward to as you keep refining your budget.

4.20 Chapter Summary

- **Budgeting = A Money Plan**: It helps you see how much you earn, how much you spend, and where you can save.
- **Choose a Method That Works**: From the 50/30/20 rule to envelope systems, pick a budgeting style that fits your life.
- **Review Regularly**: Budgets are not static; adjust them to reflect changes in income or expenses.
- **Balance Needs, Wants, and Savings**: An effective budget accounts for all three and keeps them in check.
- **Keep the Bigger Vision in Mind**: A budget is a practical tool that leads you to your financial goals, step by step.

4.21 Conclusion

Budgets may seem tedious at first, but they are one of the most powerful ways to take control of your financial life. By understanding where your money goes and making a plan for each dollar, you reduce wasteful spending and increase savings. Over time, a well-managed budget helps you build confidence and move closer to the future you have envisioned. In the next chapters, you will learn even more about handling debt and setting up an emergency fund, both of which tie neatly into the budgeting and saving habits you have started here.

CHAPTER 5: MANAGING AND REDUCING DEBT

5.1 Understanding Debt and Why It Matters

Debt occurs when you borrow money and promise to pay it back later, usually with interest. This interest is the extra fee you pay to the lender for the privilege of using their money. While some debts—like a home mortgage—can be useful, others—like high-interest credit card debt—can create significant financial stress. Learning to manage and reduce your debts is an essential skill for building a stable financial life.

Why does debt matter so much? Because every dollar you pay toward interest is a dollar that could have been used for saving, investing, or spending on something you truly need. If debt grows out of control, it can limit your choices in life. It may stop you from making a career change or starting a small business because you must focus on constant debt payments. By dealing with debt wisely, you gain freedom to shape your future.

5.2 The Different Types of Debt

Not all debt is the same. Here are some common types:

1. **Credit Card Debt**: This is one of the most widespread forms of debt. Credit cards typically have high interest rates. If you carry a balance from month to month, the interest charges can add up quickly.
2. **Student Loans**: These loans are used to pay for education. Interest rates vary, and the repayment terms can be more flexible, especially if the loans are government-backed. However, missing payments or ignoring these loans can lead to serious long-term problems.
3. **Mortgages**: A mortgage is a loan to buy a house. Mortgage interest rates are usually lower than credit card rates, and the repayment term can be long, such as 15 or 30 years. Owning a home can be a good investment, but it also comes with responsibilities like property taxes and maintenance.
4. **Car Loans**: Many people borrow money to buy a car. Interest rates depend on your credit score and the terms of the lender. Cars tend to

lose value quickly, so large car loans can become a burden if the car's worth drops below what you still owe.
5. **Personal Loans**: These can be unsecured (no collateral) or secured (backed by an asset). People use personal loans for various reasons, like consolidating other debts or covering big expenses. Interest rates vary widely.
6. **Medical Debt**: Health care costs can be very high, and sometimes people end up owing money to hospitals or clinics. Medical debt can carry its own challenges, including the possibility of negotiating a payment plan.

Understanding your specific debt types is the first step in handling them properly. Each debt has different interest rates, minimum payments, and possible consequences if you do not pay on time.

5.3 "Good Debt" vs. "Bad Debt"

Some people label certain debts as "good" or "bad." This is a simple way to separate debts that might help you build wealth from those that drain your finances with nothing in return.

- **Good Debt**: Often associated with an investment that could grow over time, such as a mortgage for a house (because property can increase in value) or a student loan (because education can help you earn more money).
- **Bad Debt**: Usually linked to items that lose value quickly, generate high interest costs, or do not contribute positively to your financial future—credit card balances for everyday purchases, payday loans, or debt taken on purely for luxury items.

Keep in mind that even so-called "good debt" can cause stress if it is more than you can handle. On the other hand, some "bad debt" might be necessary in an emergency situation. The real goal is to keep debt under control so it does not hurt your overall financial well-being.

5.4 Hidden Dangers of High-Interest Debt

High-interest debt can act like a financial black hole, sucking up your resources quickly. For instance, if you have a credit card charging 20% or more in interest each year, you could be paying hundreds of dollars extra. This makes it harder to build savings or invest for the future.

High-interest debt can also impact your credit score if you miss payments or max out your available credit. A lower credit score leads to higher interest rates on future loans, creating a cycle that is hard to escape. That is why focusing on reducing high-interest balances first is often the smartest strategy.

5.5 Finding Motivation to Pay Off Debt

Paying off debt can sometimes feel like a long, uphill battle. It helps to have a strong reason to stay motivated. Maybe you want to free up your monthly income so you can save for a home, travel, or start a family. Or perhaps you simply want to ease financial stress. When you remind yourself of the benefits—like peace of mind and the ability to use your money how *you* choose—you have a stronger drive to stick to your plan.

Some people find it motivating to imagine life after debt. Think of how it will feel not to watch a big chunk of your paycheck go to credit card bills or student loans each month. Visualizing your debt-free life can keep you going when the process seems slow.

5.6 Creating a Personal Debt Reduction Plan

A clear plan makes debt payoff more manageable. Here is a step-by-step approach:

1. **List All Debts**: Write down each debt, including the total amount owed, the interest rate, and the minimum monthly payment. This gives you a snapshot of where you stand.
2. **Prioritize**: Decide which debt to tackle first. Often, people choose the one with the highest interest rate. Others pick the smallest balance to achieve a quick win. Either way, pick a strategy and stick with it.
3. **Allocate Extra Money**: After covering your monthly bills and basic needs, direct any extra cash toward your priority debt. Keep paying the minimums on your other debts. This method allows you to focus heavily on one debt at a time.
4. **Automate Payments**: If possible, set up automatic payments so you are never late. This avoids additional fees and helps protect your credit score.

5. **Track Progress**: Regularly update a spreadsheet or simple chart to see how much your total debt load is shrinking. Seeing those numbers go down can be very motivating.
6. **Celebrate Milestones**: Each time you pay off a debt, celebrate in a modest way. Maybe treat yourself to a small reward—nothing that sets you back into more debt, of course. These mini-celebrations keep you excited about moving forward.

5.7 The Debt Snowball Method

One popular approach for paying off debt is the **snowball method**. You list all your debts from smallest to largest, ignoring the interest rate. Then, you pay as much as you can toward the smallest debt while making minimum payments on the rest. Once the smallest is fully paid, you move to the next-smallest debt. The amount you were paying on the first debt is now added to the minimum payment of the second, which helps you pay it down faster.

Why does it work? The snowball method focuses on small victories early on. When you see a debt completely gone, you feel a rush of success. This emotional boost can help you stay on track. However, a drawback is that if your largest debt also has the highest interest rate, it might be more expensive in the long run compared to some other methods.

5.8 The Debt Avalanche Method

Another well-known strategy is the **avalanche method**. Here, you rank your debts from highest interest rate to lowest interest rate. Then you put all your extra money into paying off the debt with the highest rate first. You still make minimum payments on all other debts. Once the highest-rate debt is cleared, you move on to the next highest rate, and so on.

Why does it work? The avalanche method can save you more money in the long term because you are knocking out the most expensive debt first. However, it may take longer to see a debt completely paid off if your highest-interest debt also happens to be a large balance. Some people find it less motivating because they wait longer for that first big "I'm done!" moment.

5.9 Debt Consolidation: Pros and Cons

Debt consolidation means combining multiple debts into one loan or one balance. The goal is often to get a lower overall interest rate or to simplify payment schedules. For example, you might transfer multiple credit card balances to a single new card that offers a lower rate, or you might take out a personal loan to pay off all smaller debts.

- **Pros**: You might reduce your interest costs, making it easier to pay off the total amount. Having only one payment can also lower stress and reduce the chance of missing due dates.
- **Cons**: There might be fees, like balance transfer fees or loan origination fees. Also, if you do not address the spending habits that led to debt in the first place, you might end up accumulating new balances on your old credit cards again.

Before consolidating, do your research. Compare interest rates, fees, and terms. Sometimes, sticking to an existing debt payoff plan is simpler and cheaper than taking on a new loan.

5.10 Negotiating with Creditors

Many people do not realize they can negotiate with creditors. Sometimes lenders will lower your interest rate or waive certain fees if you call and ask politely, especially if you have been a customer in good standing for a long time. They want to keep your business, so it does not hurt to try. You can also negotiate payment plans if you are temporarily unable to meet your obligations.

Negotiation is not always successful, but you might be surprised how often companies are willing to work out a better deal rather than see you default. Remember: always be polite but firm when discussing your circumstances. Explain your situation clearly and be ready to show you are committed to paying down what you owe.

5.11 Debt Management Plans and Credit Counseling

If you feel overwhelmed, you can look into professional help from non-profit credit counseling organizations. They may assist you in creating a **debt management plan** (DMP). A counselor will review your debts, income, and expenses, then contact your creditors to negotiate lower interest rates or better repayment terms. You will then make a single monthly payment to the credit counseling agency, which distributes the funds to your lenders.

- **Advantages**: You gain structure and possibly lower interest rates or fees. It can also relieve the stress of dealing with multiple creditors.
- **Disadvantages**: You may have to close your credit card accounts while on the plan, and it may affect your credit report. Plus, be sure you choose a reputable, non-profit agency.

5.12 Avoiding New Debt

Reducing existing debt is important, but so is avoiding new debt. Otherwise, you might just be treading water. Simple steps can help:

1. **Use Cash or Debit for Everyday Purchases**: This way, you do not spend money you do not have.
2. **Set a Waiting Period for Large Buys**: If you see something expensive you want, wait a few days. This helps you decide if you truly need it.
3. **Keep Credit Card Balances Low**: If you must use a credit card, aim to pay off the balance in full each month.
4. **Build an Emergency Fund**: Having a cushion for surprises prevents you from turning to credit cards when an unexpected bill arrives (more on this in Chapter 6).

Cultivating responsible spending habits is often the difference between staying out of debt and getting pulled back in.

5.13 The Mental Side of Paying Off Debt

Debt can be stressful. It weighs on your mind, making you worry about the future. Some people feel shame or embarrassment about their debt, which can lead them to hide their struggles and delay seeking help. Recognizing that debt does not define your worth as a person is crucial. Many people face debt challenges, and it is possible to overcome them with patience and the right strategies.

Staying positive helps. You might keep a journal to track how you feel as you progress. Talk to a trusted friend or family member if you need support. Some people even join online communities or groups dedicated to debt payoff, sharing tips and experiences.

5.14 Monitoring Your Credit Score

Your **credit score** is a numerical rating that lenders use to gauge how likely you are to repay debt on time. The score is influenced by factors like payment history, amount owed, length of credit history, types of credit, and new credit inquiries. Managing debt wisely can help raise your credit score. Late or missed payments, on the other hand, can harm it.

Keeping an eye on your credit score is wise. You can get free copies of your credit report each year from major reporting agencies (depending on your country). If you spot any errors—like a debt you already paid or an incorrect late payment—address it promptly by contacting the credit bureau. A healthy credit score can make a big difference in getting better interest rates when you need to borrow in the future.

5.15 Rebuilding Credit After Setbacks

If you have damaged your credit score due to missed payments or default, do not lose hope. Rebuilding credit takes time, but it is doable:

- **Make All Payments on Time**: Even one missed payment can set you back, so be consistent.
- **Pay Down Existing Balances**: This shows you are serious about reducing your total debt load.
- **Avoid Closing Old Accounts Too Soon**: Length of credit history matters. Keep older, positive accounts open to show stability.
- **Use a Secured Credit Card if Necessary**: A secured card requires a cash deposit that becomes your credit limit. It can be a stepping stone to restoring your credit if used responsibly.

Over months or years of good behavior, you will likely see your credit score climb. It will not happen overnight, but the effort can pay off in lower interest rates and easier access to financial opportunities.

5.16 Maintaining Momentum Over Time

Paying off debt is not a one-week project. It often takes months or years. That is why it helps to keep your eyes on the prize. Regularly remind yourself of why you are on this journey. You might keep a chart on your wall that shows how the total debt is going down over time. Each time you make a payment, fill in the chart a bit more. This visual aid can be fun and satisfying.

Another tip is to "pay yourself" small rewards. For instance, once you clear a specific loan, you might allow yourself a modest treat—something affordable that does not start a new cycle of debt. These little celebrations can rejuvenate your dedication to your end goal.

5.17 Creating a Debt-Free Lifestyle

When you finally clear your debts, you may feel like a huge weight has lifted from your shoulders. But the journey does not end there. Maintaining a debt-free or low-debt lifestyle involves:

1. **Spending Wisely**: Keep track of your budget to ensure you are not slipping into old habits.
2. **Saving First**: Make saving a priority—automate it if you can.
3. **Using Credit Cards with Care**: If you use them, pay off balances in full each month to avoid interest.
4. **Building an Emergency Fund**: So that you do not rely on credit cards for sudden expenses (our next chapter will dive deeper into this).

A debt-free lifestyle gives you more freedom to invest, save for retirement, or spend on experiences that truly matter to you. It can also reduce the day-to-day stress that comes with juggling multiple loan payments.

5.18 Pitfalls to Avoid

Be aware of mistakes that can derail your debt-free journey:

- **Adding New Charges to Paid-Off Accounts**: If you eliminate one debt, do not celebrate by racking up another. This undoes all your hard work.
- **Skipping Savings**: It might feel smart to put every spare penny into debt payments, but do not forget to keep at least a small emergency fund. Otherwise, a surprise expense will send you back into debt.

- **Falling for Scams**: Some companies promise to "erase your debt" instantly or charge high fees for services you can handle yourself (like negotiating interest rates). Always do careful research and consider free or reputable non-profit resources first.

5.19 Chapter Summary

1. **Know Your Debts**: List them, understand interest rates, and choose a repayment order.
2. **Pick a Strategy**: The snowball method for quick wins or avalanche method for long-term savings on interest—either can work if you stick to it.
3. **Stay Motivated**: Remind yourself of the freedom you will gain once your debt is gone. Use small milestones and visual aids.
4. **Maintain Good Habits**: Avoid new debt, watch your spending, and think carefully before taking on loans in the future.
5. **Seek Help If Needed**: Consider credit counseling or debt management if you feel overwhelmed.

5.20 Conclusion

Managing and reducing debt can transform your financial life. It is not just about numbers—it is about reducing stress, gaining control of your money, and opening up possibilities you might have closed off before. Whether you prefer the snowball or avalanche method, the most important thing is to start. Each payment you make is a step toward a future where you decide how to use your money, rather than letting debt dictate your choices.

CHAPTER 6: BUILDING AN EMERGENCY FUND FOR PEACE OF MIND

6.1 Why You Need an Emergency Fund

An emergency fund is a special pool of money you set aside for unexpected costs. These might include medical bills, urgent home or car repairs, or even sudden job loss. Without a financial cushion, you may have to rely on credit cards or loans to get through tough times. That can lead to accumulating high-interest debt and increasing stress. An emergency fund, on the other hand, offers stability and peace of mind.

Consider this scenario: your car breaks down right after your paycheck is used up for rent and bills. If you have no savings, you might have to charge the repair on a credit card at 20% interest. This debt can linger for months or even years. However, if you have an emergency fund, you can pay for the repair without going into debt and then work on replenishing the fund.

6.2 Deciding on the Right Emergency Fund Size

Opinions differ on how much money you should keep in an emergency fund. Common advice is to save **three to six months of your living expenses**. If you are single with fewer financial obligations, you might lean toward three months. If you have a family or uncertain job situation, you might aim for six or even more months. The choice depends on your comfort level, job stability, and other factors.

If saving three months of expenses sounds daunting, do not worry. Start smaller. Even $500 or $1,000 can make a big difference in handling small surprises. Over time, as you build better money habits, you can grow that safety net. The key is to start with a manageable goal, such as $1,000, and then increase it step by step.

6.3 Where to Keep Your Emergency Fund

Picking the right place to store your emergency savings is important. You want it to be accessible, but not so easily accessible that you are tempted to spend it on non-emergencies. Common choices include:

1. **High-Yield Savings Account**: This is a separate account that pays more interest than a normal checking account. It is typically easy to withdraw funds in a few days if needed, but not so quick that you will grab the money for everyday spending.
2. **Money Market Account**: Similar to a savings account, but may have certain balance requirements. It can also pay a bit more interest, and it might provide limited check-writing abilities.
3. **Certificate of Deposit (CD)**: This option usually offers a higher interest rate, but your money is locked in for a set term. Many people skip CDs for emergency funds because they want immediate access. However, some shorter-term or no-penalty CDs can work if you read the fine print.

Keep in mind that the main purpose of your emergency fund is safety and liquidity—not high returns. You do not want to invest this money in stocks or risky assets, because a market downturn could reduce its value right when you need it the most.

6.4 Getting Started with a Starter Fund

If you have never had an emergency fund, the idea of saving several months' worth of expenses might seem overwhelming. A good approach is to create a **starter fund**—often $500 to $1,000—to handle small shocks. Set aside a small sum each time you get paid until you hit your first goal. This can protect you from minor financial hiccups, like a car repair or a medical copay.

Once you reach that initial amount, do not stop. Gradually increase your goal to one month of expenses, then two, and so on. Breaking it into stages keeps you motivated and shows you that reaching these targets is possible with consistent effort.

6.5 Adding to Your Emergency Fund Regularly

To build your emergency fund, make saving automatic. Much like with other financial goals, you can set up a recurring transfer from your checking account to your emergency account right after you get paid. If it is out of sight, you are less likely to spend it. Treat your fund like a bill that must be paid—only you are paying yourself for future protection.

If your income varies, try to save a percentage of whatever comes in. For instance, decide that 10% of each paycheck or payment you receive will go straight to the emergency fund. During higher-earning months, your savings will be greater. During lower-earning months, you can still save something, keeping the habit alive.

6.6 Times to Use Your Emergency Fund

When is it okay to dip into this special reserve? The key word is *emergency*. Genuine emergencies usually share these characteristics:

1. **Unexpected**: You did not know it was coming, like a sudden illness or a layoff.
2. **Urgent**: It must be dealt with immediately, such as a leaking roof or a broken water heater in the winter.
3. **Necessary**: You cannot avoid or postpone it without serious consequences.

A sale on a new TV, for example, does not count as an emergency, even if it feels like a rare deal. Likewise, wanting to go on vacation is not an emergency (unless it is a critical family matter). By reserving your emergency fund for true needs, you ensure it is there when you have no other option.

6.7 Replenishing the Fund After Use

If you do have to use some or all of your emergency fund, make it a priority to rebuild it as soon as you can. That might mean temporarily cutting back on other budget areas or finding extra income sources. You never know when another surprise might arise. Keeping your emergency fund healthy protects you from getting stuck in high-interest debt once again.

6.8 Emotional and Mental Benefits

Having a financial safety net does more than protect your wallet. It can also reduce anxiety and improve your overall well-being. Many people have trouble sleeping if they live paycheck to paycheck and know that a single car problem could derail their entire month. An emergency fund can relieve much of that worry, giving you a sense of control over your finances.

Additionally, when you know you have enough saved to handle life's curveballs, you might feel more comfortable exploring new opportunities. You might decide to change jobs, go back to school, or even start a small business, because you are not paralyzed by the fear of what happens if something goes wrong financially.

6.9 Combining Debt Repayment with Building an Emergency Fund

A common question is whether you should focus on paying off debt first or building an emergency fund first. The truth is, you usually need to do both at the same time—but with priority. High-interest debt can be very costly, so you want to pay it down quickly. However, if you have no savings and an emergency strikes, you risk piling on more debt.

One strategy is to put a small initial amount into the emergency fund—maybe $500 or $1,000—while also making extra payments on your highest-interest debt. Once your debt is more manageable or paid off, shift those debt-payment dollars into boosting your emergency fund to the three-to-six-month range.

6.10 Strategies to Grow Your Emergency Fund Faster

If you want to speed up the process, consider these tactics:

1. **Cut Unnecessary Spending**: For a short period, try to reduce or pause certain expenses like streaming services, dining out, or subscription boxes. Put the saved money into your fund.
2. **Sell Unused Items**: Have a yard sale or use online marketplaces to sell stuff you no longer need. The cash can give your emergency savings an immediate boost.
3. **Side Hustles**: Pick up part-time work, freelance gigs, or any skill-based tasks that let you earn extra income. Funnel most of these earnings directly into the fund.
4. **Tax Refund or Bonus**: If you get a tax refund or work bonus, consider using a large part of it to supercharge your emergency account.

Small sacrifices for a few months can lead to major financial stability down the road. The goal is to fill your emergency fund as efficiently as possible without completely draining your day-to-day budget.

6.11 Avoiding Common Pitfalls

Even with the best intentions, some people struggle to build or maintain an emergency fund. Watch out for these common pitfalls:

- **Treating It Like a Regular Savings Account**: Mixing everyday savings with your emergency fund can cause confusion and lead you to spend the money on non-emergencies. Keep them separate.
- **Waiting Too Long to Start**: Some folks think, "I'll start when I make more money." But life's emergencies do not wait. Even if you can only save a small amount now, begin immediately.
- **Overfunding While Neglecting Other Goals**: If you focus only on amassing an emergency fund and ignore high-interest debt or retirement savings, you might pay more in interest or lose out on potential long-term gains. Balance is key.

6.12 Sinking Funds vs. Emergency Funds

A **sinking fund** is a separate pot of money for predictable but not monthly expenses—like car registration, holiday gifts, or annual insurance premiums. A sinking fund differs from an emergency fund because you know that expense is coming eventually. By saving a little each month, you are prepared when the bill arrives.

Your emergency fund, on the other hand, is for unforeseen costs. Mixing the two can lead to confusion. If you pull from your emergency fund to cover predictable expenses, you risk leaving yourself vulnerable in a real crisis. That is why many people choose to have multiple labeled accounts: one for emergencies, and others for planned but irregular expenses.

6.13 Real-Life Examples of Emergency Funds in Action

Maria's Story: Maria lives alone and works as a freelance graphic designer. She used to keep no savings, always relying on credit whenever a surprise popped up. After a large medical bill nearly sank her finances, she decided to build at least a two-month emergency fund. She began transferring $100 weekly into a high-yield savings account. After several months, she had $2,400 saved—enough to cover her rent and basic bills for about a month if her freelance work dried up.

She felt more confident, and when she had a minor car repair, she handled it without adding new debt.

Kevin and Nina's Story: Kevin and Nina have two children. Their car's transmission broke unexpectedly, and the repair cost $1,500. Fortunately, they had saved $3,000 in an emergency fund. They paid for the repair and then set a plan to replenish the fund with an extra $100 a month until it returned to $3,000. They avoided taking on new credit card debt and still had a cushion for other surprises.

6.14 Making the Fund Non-Negotiable

One way to ensure success is to treat your emergency fund like a mandatory expense. If you view it as optional, you may skip contributions whenever something else seems more appealing. A strong mindset says, "I must contribute to my emergency fund each paycheck, just like I pay my electric bill or rent." By giving your future self this level of importance, you develop a habit that lasts.

6.15 Balancing Emergency Savings with Other Financial Goals

Along with your emergency fund, you may have other ambitions—like paying off loans or saving for a down payment on a home. How do you balance these goals? One suggestion is to split your savings rate. For example, if you can afford to save $400 a month, maybe $200 goes to your emergency fund and $200 goes to your other goal. That way, you are making progress in both areas.

However, if you are in a high-risk situation—like an unstable job market—focusing on building a larger emergency fund first might be wiser. Each person's situation is unique, so think about which stage of financial security you are in and adjust accordingly.

6.16 Keeping the Fund Accessible Yet Safe

It is crucial that you can access your emergency money fairly quickly when a real crisis occurs—like a broken water pipe. However, you do not want to keep large sums of cash under your mattress or in your everyday checking account, because that might tempt you to use it for non-emergencies. That is why online savings accounts or money market accounts are popular. They often take a day or two for transfers, which is fast enough for most emergencies but not so instantaneous that you will dip into it on a whim.

6.17 Reviewing and Adjusting the Fund Over Time

Life changes can impact how much you need in your emergency fund. If you switch jobs, have a child, or move to a more expensive city, your monthly costs may change. That means you might need a bigger (or occasionally smaller) reserve. Review your fund at least once a year, and see if it still meets your needs. If your expenses go up, plan to adjust your contributions until your emergency fund amount reflects the higher cost of living.

6.18 Getting Family Members on Board

If you share finances with a partner or spouse, it is vital that you both agree on the importance of an emergency fund. Sit down and discuss how much you want to save, how you will save it, and under what circumstances you can tap into it. This communication can prevent disagreements later when an expense crops up. Involving older children can also teach them about financial readiness from a young age.

6.19 The Mental Aspect of Preparedness

Beyond the financial side, there is a mental aspect to having an emergency fund: it fosters a sense of being ready for life's unpredictable nature. Instead of living in fear of what might go wrong, you build confidence. You know you have at least some resources to handle the problem. This mental shift can improve other parts of your life, too, because you are not constantly looking over your shoulder for the next crisis.

6.20 Avoiding Overconfidence

While having a robust emergency fund is great, be careful not to become overconfident and neglect other priorities. It is possible to save too much in a low-interest emergency account while ignoring investment opportunities or paying off debt. If you have, for example, a year's worth of expenses sitting in a 1% interest account but you are paying 10% on a credit card, you might be losing more than you are saving. Always maintain balance. Once you have a comfortable cushion, consider directing surplus funds into debt reduction or diversified investments.

6.21 Chapter Summary

1. **Emergency Fund = Safety Net**: This pool of money is for genuine surprises.
2. **Starting Small Is Fine**: Even $500 to $1,000 can prevent you from turning to high-interest credit during minor setbacks.
3. **Automate and Separate**: Make regular transfers into a distinct account so you are not tempted to spend.
4. **Use It Only for Real Emergencies**: Repairs, medical bills, or job loss are typical valid reasons. A sale on electronics is not.
5. **Replenish After Use**: Do not forget to rebuild the fund once you dip into it.

6.22 Conclusion

Building an emergency fund is one of the most impactful moves you can make for your financial security. It protects you from life's sudden costs and allows you to face challenges without panic or resorting to expensive debt. As you continue to grow in your financial knowledge and discipline, keep your emergency fund a top priority. Whether it is a starter fund or several months of living expenses, having that safety net can provide a level of calm and confidence that money alone does not always buy.

CHAPTER 7: BASICS OF INVESTING AND GROWING YOUR MONEY

7.1 Introduction: Why Invest?

Up to this point, we have discussed saving, budgeting, and handling debt. These are crucial steps to achieve financial security. But once you have a stable foundation—your emergency fund is in place, and you have some savings—it is time to consider how to make your money grow. That is where **investing** comes in.

Investing is the act of using your money to buy assets (like stocks, bonds, or real estate) that have the potential to earn you more money over time. The main reason people invest is to outpace inflation and build wealth. Inflation is the increase in prices of goods and services over time. If your money only sits in a regular bank account with very low interest, it may lose value in the long run because of inflation. On the other hand, investing gives your money a chance to earn higher returns. Of course, returns are never guaranteed, and investing involves risk. Still, many see investing as the most practical way to grow wealth over the long term.

7.2 Saving vs. Investing

It is important to distinguish between *saving* and *investing*. Saving usually means placing your money in a safe and accessible location—like a savings account—where you can easily get it if an emergency happens. You should keep your emergency fund in this type of low-risk account. But the trade-off is that your money usually grows more slowly there.

Investing, however, means accepting some level of risk in exchange for higher potential returns. Historically, markets such as the stock market have grown over the long run, but there are ups and downs along the way. That is why investing is typically recommended for goals at least five years away—like retirement, buying a home in the future, or funding a child's education. You can weather the market's short-term storms while you aim for long-term gains.

7.3 The Concept of Risk and Return

When you invest, you take on *risk*, which is the possibility that the value of your investment could go down. But with higher risk often comes the potential for higher reward—or higher *return*. A return is the gain (or loss) you experience from your investment. It can come from an increase in the asset's value (like a stock price going up) or from income the asset produces (such as dividend payments or interest).

Here is a simple way to think of risk and return:

- **Low Risk, Low Return**: A savings account or certificate of deposit (CD) is considered very safe, but the interest you earn might be modest.
- **Moderate Risk, Moderate Return**: Bonds, some real estate projects, or balanced mutual funds can offer steady growth with moderate risk.
- **High Risk, High Return**: Stocks of new companies, certain business ventures, or specialized real estate projects can yield big gains, but they can also lose value quickly.

Your comfort with risk—often called your **risk tolerance**—is personal. Some people are okay with bigger ups and downs because they aim for higher returns over time. Others would rather sleep better at night with more stable investments, even if they earn less.

7.4 Common Investment Options

There are many ways to invest. Below are some basics:

1. **Stocks (Equities)**: When you buy a share of a company's stock, you become a part-owner (shareholder) of that company. If the company does well, the stock price may rise, allowing you to sell at a profit. Some companies also pay dividends. The risk is that the stock price can drop if the company performs poorly or if the market declines overall.
2. **Bonds (Fixed Income)**: Buying a bond means lending money to a government or a corporation. In return, they pay you interest on a set schedule, and when the bond "matures," you get the original amount back. Bonds are generally considered more stable than stocks, but they usually offer smaller returns.

3. **Mutual Funds**: These are investment funds that pool money from many investors to buy a diversified mix of stocks, bonds, or other assets. A professional manager decides which assets to buy and sell. Mutual funds can be an easy way to invest in many different companies at once.
4. **Index Funds**: A type of mutual fund (or Exchange-Traded Fund, ETF) that tries to match the performance of a market index like the S&P 500. Instead of a manager picking stocks, the fund automatically invests in the same companies that are in the index. These funds often have lower fees than actively managed mutual funds.
5. **Exchange-Traded Funds (ETFs)**: Similar to mutual funds, but they trade like stocks on an exchange. You can buy or sell an ETF at any point during the trading day. Many ETFs track an index, while others target specific industries or strategies.
6. **Real Estate**: Some people buy houses or other properties to rent or sell for profit. This can be a long-term investment, but it requires maintenance, taxes, and other costs. Alternatively, you can invest in real estate investment trusts (REITs), which own and manage properties on behalf of shareholders.
7. **Retirement Accounts**: In many countries, special accounts (like 401(k) or IRA in the U.S.) offer tax benefits to encourage long-term investing. These accounts hold your investments until retirement age, when you can start withdrawing. The main advantage is tax deferral or tax-free growth, depending on the type of account.

7.5 Diversification: Not Putting All Eggs in One Basket

One of the golden rules of investing is **diversification**. This means spreading your money across different types of assets—like a mix of stocks, bonds, and perhaps some real estate—so that if one area performs poorly, your entire portfolio does not suffer as much.

Think of it like this: if you invest all your money in just one company's stock, and that company does poorly, you lose a big chunk of your portfolio value. But if you spread your investment across dozens or hundreds of companies—often through mutual funds or index funds—you reduce the risk that any single company's performance will ruin your overall returns.

7.6 Setting Clear Investment Goals

Before jumping into investments, it helps to outline why you are investing. Are you saving for retirement? A child's college fund? A dream home in ten years? A new business venture someday? Having clear goals can guide your investment choices. For example, a retirement portfolio might focus more on index funds and stable growth over decades, while saving for a down payment in five years might require investments that are somewhat stable and easier to convert into cash when you need them.

Having a specific timeline also matters. Money you need soon (one to three years) might be safer in low-risk or more liquid options. Money you will not need for 20 years can handle more market fluctuations because it has time to recover from downturns.

7.7 Getting Started with Investing

How do you actually begin? Here is a simple roadmap:

1. **Check Your Financial Foundation**: Make sure you have paid down high-interest debt (like credit cards) and built an emergency fund. High-interest debt can cost you more than you might earn from typical investments.
2. **Choose a Brokerage or Platform**: You will need an account where you can buy and sell investments. Many banks and financial firms offer brokerage services. There are also user-friendly apps for new investors.
3. **Start Small**: You do not need huge sums of money to begin. Some platforms let you invest with $50 or $100. You can often buy fractions of shares. The key is to start and learn as you go.
4. **Pick an Investment Strategy**: Many beginners start with broad index funds because they are simpler and more diversified. You can add more specialized investments once you gain confidence.
5. **Automate Contributions**: If possible, set up an automatic transfer from your checking account into your investment account. This approach—sometimes called "paying yourself first"—helps you invest regularly without trying to time the market.

7.8 Understanding Fees and Expenses

Investing is not free. Different funds or brokerage services charge various fees. Over a long period, high fees can reduce your returns significantly. For example, mutual funds might have an expense ratio (a yearly fee based on the amount you have invested). Some brokers charge transaction fees for buying or selling. Index funds and ETFs generally have lower fees compared to actively managed funds.

What should you look for?

- **Expense Ratio**: Aim for funds with an expense ratio under 1%, preferably under 0.5%. Some index funds even offer ratios under 0.1%.
- **Trading Fees**: Make sure you are aware of any commissions for buying or selling. Some brokerages offer commission-free trades on stocks or ETFs.
- **Account Maintenance Fees**: Some platforms charge monthly or annual fees just for having an account. Look for options that waive these fees, especially for smaller balances.

7.9 Emotional Traps: Avoiding Fear and Greed

A big part of investing is managing your emotions. When markets rise rapidly, some people get overly excited and invest aggressively, only to face losses when a correction happens. When markets drop, fear can lead others to panic-sell at a low price, locking in losses instead of waiting for a rebound. These emotional decisions can seriously hurt long-term returns.

An effective way to avoid emotional traps is to stick to a plan. If you are investing with a 10- or 20-year timeline, day-to-day market swings do not matter as much. Taking a long view usually means staying calm during short-term dips and not chasing quick profits during booms.

7.10 Reinvesting Earnings

One of the great benefits of investing is that returns can generate more returns, especially if you reinvest them. If a stock or mutual fund pays you dividends, you can use that cash to buy more shares instead of spending it. This process feeds into the power of *compound growth*, which we will explore even more in Chapter 8.

For example, say you have a mutual fund that pays a dividend of $50. If you reinvest that $50 into more shares of the fund, the next time it pays a dividend, you own a bit more, so you get a slightly bigger payout. Over years or decades, this can significantly boost your overall returns.

7.11 Monitoring and Rebalancing

Investing is not a "set it and forget it" activity—though you also do not need to check your account every day. A good balance might be reviewing your portfolio a few times a year to ensure it still reflects your goals and comfort with risk. Over time, certain investments may perform better than others, causing your portfolio to become uneven. For instance, your stock holdings might grow a lot, making up a larger portion of your investments than you originally planned.

Rebalancing involves selling some of the investments that have become too large a part of your portfolio and buying others that have shrunk. This helps keep your risk level consistent with your original plan. If, for example, you want to maintain a 70% stocks, 30% bonds mix, and after a big stock market rally you find yourself at 80% stocks, 20% bonds, you might sell some stocks and buy more bonds.

7.12 Avoiding Get-Rich-Quick Schemes

Investing is a long-term strategy, not a quick money-making trick. Be wary of schemes promising huge returns in a short time. Many of these are high-risk gambles or outright scams. A big red flag is someone guaranteeing you a large return with no risk—because all investing carries some risk.

Other signs of a possible scam include pressure to invest "right now," overly complicated explanations, or a lack of transparent information about fees and track records. A good principle is: if it sounds too good to be true, it probably is.

7.13 Investing for Retirement

For many people, retirement is the biggest investing goal. Retirement accounts offer tax advantages that can supercharge your savings. Depending on your country, these accounts may allow your money to grow tax-free or tax-deferred, meaning you pay taxes later when you withdraw. If your employer offers a matching contribution—like contributing an amount equal to some portion of your own contribution—take advantage of it. That is essentially free money for you.

Because retirement investing typically spans many years or decades, you can afford to take on a bit more risk (such as investing in a higher percentage of stocks) when you are younger. As you get closer to retirement age, you might shift to more conservative choices like bonds or stable value funds to protect what you have accumulated.

7.14 Socially Responsible Investing

Some investors also care about the social or environmental impact of the companies they invest in. **Socially Responsible Investing (SRI)** or **Environmental, Social, and Governance (ESG)** funds focus on businesses that meet certain ethical guidelines. For instance, they might avoid tobacco or fossil fuel companies, or focus on clean energy and fair labor practices.

While the primary goal of investing is often financial gain, some people feel more comfortable placing their money where it aligns with their personal values. Keep in mind, however, that there is no universal standard for what counts as "socially responsible," so research is important if this area interests you.

7.15 Common Investing Mistakes to Avoid

1. **Trying to Time the Market**: Many people attempt to guess the market's highs and lows, only to miss out on the best days or sell at the worst times. A steady, long-term approach often works better.
2. **Not Diversifying Enough**: Putting all your money into one stock or one type of investment can lead to large losses if that asset performs poorly.
3. **Ignoring Fees**: High fees eat away at your returns over time. Always check expense ratios and transaction fees.
4. **Panic Selling**: Markets move in cycles. A big drop can feel scary, but if you sell too soon, you might lock in losses that could have recovered.
5. **Failing to Rebalance**: Over time, your investments might become too skewed toward one asset class. Rebalancing helps manage risk.
6. **Investing Without a Plan**: It is easier to make emotional choices when you do not have clear goals. Know why you are investing and what timeline you have in mind.

7.16 Long-Term vs. Short-Term Investing

Short-term investing (or trading) aims to make a profit within days, weeks, or months. It can be very risky, especially for beginners, because stock prices can fluctuate wildly in the short run. Long-term investing generally refers to holding assets for multiple years or even decades. Over time, the market's upward trend can work in your favor, despite dips and downturns along the way.

For most people working regular jobs who do not have the time or desire to study market trends daily, a long-term approach is less stressful and often more successful. Short-term trading usually requires constant monitoring, in-depth market research, and a high tolerance for losing money.

7.17 Staying Educated

Investing is not something you learn once and never revisit. The financial world changes all the time. You can keep learning through:

- **Books and Articles**: Many free resources explain market basics or advanced topics.
- **Webinars and Online Courses**: Some platforms offer beginner-friendly courses on how to pick investments, manage risk, or read financial statements.
- **Professional Advice**: A certified financial planner or advisor can guide you, especially if you have significant assets or complex questions. Just be sure you understand how they are paid (fees, commissions, or both).

The more you learn, the better your decisions. But do not let the fear of not knowing everything stop you from starting small. You will gain practical experience along the way.

7.18 Balancing Life and Investing

It is easy to get excited about investing and focus too heavily on it at the expense of other financial or life goals. For instance, you might want to invest aggressively but also need to fund a child's education in the near future. You might want to buy a house soon. Or you might have a personal dream like traveling the world or starting a side business.

Balancing investing with other financial priorities is key. You do not want to invest every spare cent if it means you have nothing left for emergencies or near-term goals. Similarly, you do not want to ignore long-term growth because you are spending all your money on short-term pleasures.

7.19 Tracking Your Progress

Once you begin investing, you might wonder how to measure your progress. A few ways to do this include:

- **Compare Your Returns to a Benchmark**: If you invest mostly in large U.S. companies, you might compare your results to the S&P 500 index.
- **Check Account Growth Over Time**: Are your balances steadily increasing? Even with market dips, is the trend moving up over the years?
- **Revisit Goals**: If your goal was to build a certain retirement balance by a certain year, see if you are on track.

Try not to obsess over daily or weekly returns. A monthly or quarterly review is often enough for most long-term investors.

7.20 Passing on the Investing Habit

If you have children or younger siblings, teaching them about investing can give them a huge head start. Simple lessons about saving money, explaining what stocks are, and showing them how compound interest works (which we will discuss in the next chapter) can spark an interest in long-term thinking. Even small investments made at a young age have a lot of time to grow.

By talking openly about how investing helps build security and wealth over the long term, you can encourage positive habits in your family. Let them see how you check your statements periodically, set goals, and stay patient during market ups and downs. This example can be a valuable teaching tool.

7.21 Chapter Summary

- **Investing vs. Saving**: Saving is for safety and easy access; investing is for higher potential returns over longer periods.
- **Risk and Return**: Accept some risk to seek bigger gains, but know your comfort level.

- **Diversification**: Spread your money across various investments to reduce overall risk.
- **Set Goals and Plans**: Know why you are investing (retirement, house, education, etc.) and how long you can let your money grow.
- **Start Small and Keep Learning**: You do not need a fortune to begin. Use index funds, watch fees, and stay calm during market swings.

7.22 Conclusion

Investing is a powerful way to grow your money, but it requires patience, discipline, and ongoing learning. By understanding the basics—like how stocks, bonds, and mutual funds work—you lay the groundwork for more informed decisions. With a solid plan, a clear time horizon, and a commitment to steady contributions, you can harness the potential of the financial markets to build wealth over the long haul.

CHAPTER 8: THE POWER OF COMPOUND INTEREST

8.1 What Is Compound Interest?

Compound interest is often called one of the most powerful forces in finance. It occurs when the interest you earn on your money also starts to earn interest. In other words, you are not just getting returns on your original investment—you are also getting returns on your returns. Over many years, this can lead to explosive growth.

Let us break it down with a simple example. Suppose you invest $1,000 at a yearly interest rate of 10%. By the end of the first year, you have earned $100 in interest (10% of $1,000), giving you $1,100. In the second year, you earn 10% not just on $1,000, but on the entire $1,100—so you earn $110. Now you have $1,210. In the third year, you earn 10% on $1,210, which is $121, and so on. Each year, the amount you earn in interest grows because your total balance grows.

8.2 How Compound Interest Differs from Simple Interest

Simple interest is calculated only on the original amount you invest, also known as the principal. So if you invest $1,000 at 10% simple interest, you earn $100 each year, no more. After five years, you have $1,500.

But with **compound interest**, every year you earn interest on the principal plus the accumulated interest from previous years. After five years, you would have more than $1,500. The difference may not look huge in the short term, but over 10 or 20 years, the gap can become immense.

8.3 Why Time Matters

The secret ingredient to compound interest is **time**. The earlier you start, the more powerful the compounding effect becomes. Even small contributions can become significant sums after decades. This is why many financial experts urge people to start saving and investing as soon as possible, even if it is just a little bit.

Imagine you start investing $200 a month at age 25, earning an average of 8% per year. By the time you are 65, the compounding effect could turn those monthly contributions into a substantial retirement fund. But if you wait until age 35 to start, you would have to invest much more each month to reach the same amount by 65. The lost decade means you missed out on 10 years of compounding growth.

8.4 Compounding Frequency

Compound interest can be applied on different schedules—annually, quarterly, monthly, or even daily. The more often the interest is added to your balance, the faster it grows. For example, monthly compounding will grow your money slightly faster than annual compounding at the same annual percentage rate (APR). While the difference might be small each year, it can become quite noticeable over time.

Some savings accounts offer daily compounding, meaning interest is calculated each day and added to your balance, so the next day's interest is based on the slightly higher amount. Always read the details on how often an account compounds interest when comparing options.

8.5 Examples of Compound Growth

Let us look at a hypothetical scenario:

- **Initial Investment**: $5,000
- **Annual Contribution**: $2,000 (added each year)
- **Annual Interest Rate**: 8%
- **Time Horizon**: 20 years

If this growth compounds annually, you might end up with around $98,000 by the end of 20 years. Now, if you find an option that compounds monthly (and effectively keeps the same 8% annual rate), the total might be a bit higher—perhaps $100,000 or more—because of that more frequent compounding.

These are rough calculations, but they show how contributions plus compounding over time can build up. The key is consistency and patience.

8.6 Compound Interest with Regular Contributions

In many cases, you will not just invest a lump sum and leave it; you will keep adding to your investments over the years—like making monthly or yearly contributions. Each new contribution has its own compounding journey. The longer each contribution stays invested, the more it can grow. Even if you can only add small amounts, those amounts stack upon each other. This is why an automatic investing habit is so powerful. You set it and forget it, and over time, you might be pleasantly surprised by how much your balance has grown.

8.7 Compound Interest and Retirement Accounts

Retirement accounts are a common place where people take advantage of compound interest. Contributions made in your 20s or 30s can have 30 or 40 years to grow. If these accounts also offer a match from your employer, you can grow your balance even faster. The combination of employer match, compound growth, and tax benefits can give your money a long runway to multiply.

But remember, if you withdraw early from certain retirement accounts, you might face penalties or extra taxes. The rules vary depending on the type of account and your country's laws. Because these accounts are designed for the long haul, you want to let that money sit and grow without interruption.

8.8 Compounding Works in Debt, Too

Compound interest can also work *against* you when it comes to high-interest debt, such as credit cards. Here, the balance you owe can grow rapidly if you only make the minimum payment. That is why managing high-interest debt is so critical—otherwise, the unpaid interest adds to your principal, and you start paying interest on the interest. This can create a cycle that is difficult to break.

For instance, if you carry $1,000 on a credit card with a 20% annual rate and only pay a small amount each month, the compounding effect makes the debt balloon, costing you far more than $1,000 over time. That is why paying off high-interest debt quickly is usually a smart financial move.

8.9 Harnessing Compound Interest in Everyday Life

Beyond traditional investing, compound interest can appear in other financial areas:

- **Savings Accounts**: Though returns are smaller compared to the stock market, many savings accounts pay compound interest. Every little bit helps.
- **Certificates of Deposit (CDs)**: These typically offer higher rates than basic savings accounts and also compound over the term of the CD.
- **Reinvesting Dividends**: If you own dividend-paying stocks or funds, automatically reinvesting dividends is a way to make compound interest work for you.

Even in personal goals not directly tied to money, the idea of compounding can be applied. For example, small efforts every day—whether in fitness, learning, or career—can add up to huge improvements over time. This is not financial compounding, but the principle is similar: consistent, steady progress can lead to exponential results down the line.

8.10 Starting Early: A Tale of Two Investors

A common illustration of compound interest's power is the story of two investors:

- **Investor A** starts investing $200 a month at age 25 and does so for 10 years, then stops contributing altogether. But they leave the money invested until age 65.
- **Investor B** waits until age 35 to start investing $200 a month and continues investing until age 65 (a full 30 years).

Surprisingly, in some scenarios, **Investor A** can end up with more money at age 65 than **Investor B**, even though Investor A only contributed for 10 years and Investor B contributed for 30. The reason is that Investor A gave their money more total years to compound. The early start made a huge difference.

While the exact numbers depend on interest rates, the lesson is clear: *time in the market* can be more important than *timing the market*.

8.11 Staying Consistent During Market Ups and Downs

One challenge with relying on compound interest is that many investments—like stocks—fluctuate in value. There will be years when the market falls, and your investment might seem to lose value. Some people get scared and sell. But if your goal is long-term growth, riding through those dips is often necessary. Historically, markets recover and continue upward over long stretches.

By steadily investing (such as monthly or quarterly) regardless of market conditions, you can benefit from *dollar-cost averaging*—buying more shares when prices are low and fewer shares when prices are high, which can smooth out your average cost over time. This constant investment approach also helps you avoid trying to predict market movements, which is extremely difficult, even for experts.

8.12 The Role of Compound Interest in Achieving Financial Freedom

Financial freedom—or the point at which you can live off your investments and other passive income—often relies heavily on compound interest. As your investments grow, they can begin to produce returns (like dividends, interest, or rent) that exceed your regular expenses. Once that happens, you are no longer *forced* to work for money; you have enough assets that your money effectively works for you.

Reaching this stage usually takes patience and planning. The earlier and more consistently you invest, the sooner you may get there. But even if you start later, compound interest can still help you achieve greater financial stability than if you did not invest at all.

8.13 Being Realistic About Returns

While compound interest can work wonders, it is also important to keep expectations realistic. Earning 7% or 8% a year over several decades might be feasible for a diversified portfolio of stocks and bonds (based on historical data), but expecting 20% or 30% returns annually is not realistic in normal circumstances.

Sticking to a reasonable outlook helps you stay committed. If you assume you will get rich overnight, you might be tempted by risky schemes or become disappointed quickly when normal market returns do not match your inflated hopes.

8.14 Using Calculators to Plan

Many financial websites have **compound interest calculators**. These tools let you plug in your initial investment, monthly contributions, estimated rate of return, and the number of years you plan to invest. Then they show you an estimate of how your money might grow over time. While these are only estimates and cannot predict the future exactly, they can give you a sense of what consistent investing can achieve.

Try adjusting different factors to see the impact:

- **If you raise your monthly contribution** by $50, how much more will you have in 20 years?
- **If you start 5 years later**, how much less will you have by retirement age?
- **If you assume 6% returns instead of 8%**, how does that change your final amount?

These calculations can help you set saving and investing goals that feel both motivating and achievable.

8.15 Fighting the Urge to Withdraw Early

Because compound interest becomes more powerful over time, you want to avoid withdrawing from your investments unless it is absolutely necessary or you have reached your intended goal (such as retirement). Every time you pull money out, you lose potential future gains on that amount. This is similar to pruning a plant just as it starts to blossom.

It is why maintaining an emergency fund and keeping your day-to-day finances in order is so essential—so you do not have to tap into your investments for small or medium financial surprises.

8.16 Compound Interest for Children and Teens

If you have children or teens, teaching them about compound interest early can give them a huge advantage. Even small sums saved from birthday money or part-time jobs can become substantial over decades. Some parents open a small investment or savings account for their kids, allowing the kids to watch the balance grow. This not only builds their net worth but also teaches valuable lessons about patience and the rewards of long-term thinking.

8.17 Compound Interest in Everyday Purchases

While compound interest is mainly discussed in investments or debt, you can also consider its spirit in everyday purchases. Think of it this way: every $100 you spend today is not just $100—it is $100 that could have been growing in an investment for 10 or 20 years. Over a long period, you might have turned that $100 into a much larger amount. This does not mean you can never spend money, but it highlights the "opportunity cost" of every dollar you use.

Sometimes, just remembering that money can grow on its own if given time can make you think twice about impulsive purchases. You might decide that future gains are worth more to you than an immediate but short-lived pleasure.

8.18 Combining Compound Interest with Other Strategies

Compound interest alone is not the entire financial picture. You still need:

- **A Solid Budget**: So you do not overspend and end up with debt that compounds negatively.
- **A Healthy Emergency Fund**: To handle life's surprises.
- **Debt Management**: Especially for high-interest debt, which compounds against you.
- **Good Earning Potential**: Through career development or side ventures to supply the money you want to invest.

When all these elements work together, compound interest can be the engine that propels you toward your most ambitious money goals.

8.19 Celebrating Milestones

Watching your investments grow via compound interest can be exciting. Set small milestones—like reaching $1,000, then $5,000, then $10,000, and beyond. Each time you hit a new level, acknowledge it. Maybe treat yourself to a modest celebration, or write a note in a journal. Recognizing progress can keep you motivated, especially since compounding is a long game and big results often take years to unfold.

8.20 Potential Pitfalls

While compound interest is powerful, here are some pitfalls to avoid:

1. **Ignoring Fees**: High fees can slow down your compounding because they drain your returns each year.
2. **Overestimating Returns**: Assuming unrealistically high interest rates can lead to disappointment.
3. **Inconsistent Contributions**: Missing contributions reduces the money you have working for you over time.
4. **Starting Too Late**: Every year you wait is a year of potential growth you will never get back.
5. **Withdrawing Early**: This interrupts compounding and can cost you a lot in long-term growth.

8.21 Chapter Summary

- **Compound Interest Basics**: Your interest earns interest, creating a snowball effect that grows bigger over time.
- **Time Is Key**: The earlier you start, the more remarkable the results can be.
- **Frequent Contributions**: Adding money regularly fuels the compounding engine.
- **Avoid Early Withdrawals**: Keep your money growing as long as you can.
- **Applies to Debt Too**: High-interest debt compounds in a harmful way, so paying it off quickly saves money.

8.22 Conclusion

Compound interest can transform small, consistent investments into a large sum over many years. It is a cornerstone of long-term wealth building, especially when combined with regular contributions, diversification, and a patient mindset. By understanding how compound interest works—and by putting it to use in retirement accounts, savings, or other investments—you can harness one of the most powerful forces in finance.

With a solid grasp of saving, budgeting, debt management, investing fundamentals, and now the magic of compounding, you are well on your way to creating lasting financial security. In the upcoming chapters, we will continue exploring how to set and track goals, spend wisely, and increase income, each of which complements the power of compound interest and helps you move closer to true financial freedom.

CHAPTER 9: DEFINING AND TRACKING FINANCIAL GOALS

9.1 Why Setting Financial Goals Matters

You have learned about having a healthy money mindset, saving, budgeting, managing debt, and investing. These lessons are strong building blocks for your financial life. But if you do not have clear goals, it is like having a car with fuel and a map but no final destination. Goals give you a place to drive toward. They help you make sense of the daily decisions about how you use, save, or invest your money.

When you set goals, you give your financial habits a purpose. You might have short-term goals like buying a new laptop or paying off a small debt. Then there are medium-term goals, such as buying a car or saving for a wedding in a few years. Finally, you have long-term goals—like purchasing a home or retiring comfortably decades from now. No matter the size or scope, goals serve as targets that keep you motivated and on track.

9.2 Types of Financial Goals

Financial goals generally fall into three categories based on the timeline you give yourself:

1. **Short-Term Goals (up to 1 year)**: These might include paying off a small credit card balance, saving for a vacation, or building a starter emergency fund. Short-term goals often require quick, decisive action and give you a sense of accomplishment sooner.
2. **Medium-Term Goals (1 to 5 years)**: Common examples are saving for a down payment on a car or funding a dream trip that is more expensive. You might also aim to clear all credit card debt or improve your credit score. Medium-term goals keep you focused on staying consistent over a few years.
3. **Long-Term Goals (5 years or more)**: These include buying a house, paying for your children's education, or building a comfortable retirement fund. Long-term goals often rely on the power of compound interest, which we

discussed in Chapter 8. They require patience and dedication over many years or even decades.

Having a mix of these three types of goals ensures you have both near-term milestones to keep you excited and big dreams to pull you forward. The short-term wins give you quick motivation, and the long-term vision reminds you why it is worth staying disciplined.

9.3 The S.M.A.R.T. Method of Goal-Setting

A popular way to set goals—financial or otherwise—is the **S.M.A.R.T.** method. This approach helps you define goals clearly:

- **S**: **Specific** – Be clear about what you want. "Save money" is too vague. "Save $5,000 for a home down payment" is specific.
- **M**: **Measurable** – You must be able to measure your progress. If your goal is to save $5,000, then you can track how much you have saved at any point.
- **A**: **Achievable** – The goal should be realistic given your income and expenses. It should stretch you a bit but not be impossible.
- **R**: **Relevant** – Make sure the goal matters to your life situation. If you do not truly care about it, you might lose interest.
- **T**: **Time-Bound** – Set a deadline. "Save $5,000 in 10 months" forces you to act. Without a time frame, you might procrastinate.

Let us say you want to build an emergency fund. A S.M.A.R.T. version of this goal could be, "I will save $1,000 in my emergency fund in six months by setting aside $167 per month." It is specific, measurable, likely achievable (assuming your budget allows), relevant to your financial security, and has a clear deadline.

9.4 Linking Goals to Your Vision

In Chapter 2, we discussed creating a clear vision for your financial future—maybe you want to own a cozy house by the beach or retire early to travel the world. Goals are the stepping stones that lead you from today's reality to that long-term vision. Each short or medium-term goal should ideally connect back to your broader dream. For instance, if your vision is homeownership, one of your goals might be, "Save 20% for a down payment within 5 years."

Linking your goals to your bigger vision can keep you inspired. On tough days when you feel tempted to skip saving, remembering your future home or early retirement plan can help you push through. It gives every dollar you save or invest a deeper meaning.

9.5 Breaking Large Goals into Smaller Steps

Some goals, especially long-term ones, might feel huge. You might want to have $500,000 in your retirement account or pay off $50,000 in student loans. Seeing that large number can feel overwhelming at first. A helpful strategy is to break these giant goals into smaller mini-goals or milestones.

For example:

- If you need $50,000 for a down payment in 5 years, you might aim to save $10,000 each year.
- That becomes about $833 a month.
- Breaking that down further, it is roughly $192 a week.

Suddenly, your massive goal feels more like a weekly task. Of course, $192 a week might still be a challenge, but it is more approachable than looking at the entire $50,000 at once. Each smaller milestone you hit can become a reason to celebrate your progress.

9.6 Tools for Tracking Goals

Once you set your goals, you need a system to **track** them. This tracking tells you how far you have come and whether you are on pace. Some people prefer low-tech solutions like a notebook or a whiteboard. Others use spreadsheets or budgeting apps. Here are some popular methods:

1. **Spreadsheet Software**: Create a separate sheet for each goal. List the target amount, monthly or weekly contributions, and the deadline. Update the balance whenever you contribute.
2. **Budgeting or Goal-Tracking Apps**: Many apps let you set specific targets, like "Vacation Fund: $2,000 by August 31." You can link your bank accounts, and the app tracks your progress automatically.
3. **Visual Thermometers or Charts**: Some people color in a savings "thermometer" on paper every time they get closer to their goal. This

old-school method can be surprisingly motivating because you see your progress in real-time.
   4. **Digital Envelopes**: If you use an envelope system (discussed in the budgeting chapter), you can have separate envelopes for each goal. Watching the money accumulate in each envelope is a tangible way to track.

The key is consistency. Pick a method you like, and update it regularly—weekly, bi-weekly, or monthly. Regular check-ins keep your goals top of mind and help you spot problems early.

9.7 Staying Motivated and Accountable

Goals can lose their shine over time, especially long-term ones that might take years to accomplish. To stay motivated:

- **Celebrate Small Wins**: If your plan is to save $5,000, do something nice (but modest) when you reach $1,000, then $2,500, and so on. Each mini-victory is an achievement worth recognizing.
- **Create Vision Boards**: A poster or digital collage of images representing your goal (like a home or a travel destination) can serve as a daily reminder.
- **Find an Accountability Partner**: Share your goal with a friend or family member who will check in on your progress. You can update them monthly and discuss any challenges.
- **Track Progress Publicly**: Some people post about their goals on social media or in online communities. The public commitment can push you to stay on track because you know others are following your journey.
- **Review Why It Matters**: Periodically remind yourself why you set this goal. What will achieving it allow you to do or feel? That deeper purpose can recharge your determination.

9.8 Handling Setbacks

Even with the best plan, life can throw curveballs. You might face a medical emergency, car repairs, or a sudden job loss. These events can slow down—or sometimes reverse—your progress. It is important to recognize that setbacks happen to everyone. They are not a sign of failure but part of the journey.

How to handle them:

1. **Revisit Your Budget**: You may need to adjust your goal contributions for a while. If you cannot save $200 a month, maybe $100 is still doable until you get back on your feet.
2. **Use Your Emergency Fund**: This is exactly why an emergency fund exists. Do not feel guilty about tapping into it. Just make a plan to replenish it once the crisis passes.
3. **Adjust Your Timeline**: If a major setback occurs, you might need to push your goal deadline out by a few months or even a year. That is okay. Better to adjust the plan than give up entirely.
4. **Seek Support**: Talk to family, friends, or a financial counselor if the setback is severe. Getting advice and emotional support can help you bounce back faster.

Remember, every challenge is a chance to learn and grow. Maybe you realize you should aim for a larger emergency fund next time or get additional insurance coverage. View setbacks as lessons, not roadblocks.

9.9 Reviewing and Updating Goals

Your financial goals are not set in stone. Over time, your life circumstances, priorities, or income may change. You might get married, have children, change careers, or relocate. Each of these events can reshape your financial picture. That is why reviewing your goals at least once a year is wise.

Ask yourself:

- Are these goals still relevant?
- Do the amounts and deadlines still make sense?
- Do I need to add new goals or remove old ones?
- Should I direct more resources to one goal and less to another?

Regular reviews keep your goals aligned with your current reality and help you avoid the drift that can happen if you set a goal once and never look at it again.

9.10 Balancing Multiple Goals

Often, you will have to juggle more than one goal at a time. Maybe you are paying off debt while saving for a wedding, and you also want to start investing for retirement. Balancing these goals involves prioritizing which ones need the most immediate attention. High-interest debt might be at the top because it costs you more every day you delay. But you might still set aside a bit of money monthly for your wedding fund or retirement contributions so you do not lose momentum.

A simple approach is to decide which goal is most urgent, then allocate more of your monthly surplus toward that goal. The others receive smaller amounts until the first goal is met. After you eliminate the top-priority goal—like clearing a specific debt—free up that money to put toward the next goal in line.

9.11 Real-Life Examples of Goal-Setting Success

Case Study 1: Miguel's Car Fund
Miguel is tired of spending too much on car repairs. He wants a newer, reliable vehicle. He sets a S.M.A.R.T. goal: "I will save $6,000 in 12 months to buy a used car by next August." Miguel breaks this down into $500 a month. He cuts back on eating out and works a few extra shifts. To keep himself motivated, he posts a picture of the car model he wants on his fridge. He tracks his savings using a spreadsheet. By next August, he has $6,000 ready, buys a used car without a loan, and celebrates a debt-free purchase.

Case Study 2: Bree's Dream of Homeownership
Bree dreams of owning a small condo. She calculates she needs $30,000 for a 20% down payment. She gives herself 4 years. That is $7,500 per year, or about $625 per month. She opens a separate high-yield savings account called "Condo Fund." Each paycheck, she automatically transfers $300 from her checking to that account. She also picks up freelance work on weekends, depositing extra earnings directly into the Condo Fund. Some months she can contribute $700; others, only $500. Yet overall, she stays close to her monthly average. After 4 years, she has the $30,000 needed and begins house-hunting.

These examples highlight that defining a clear goal and sticking to a plan can turn big ambitions into achievable realities. Both Miguel and Bree had distinct time frames, specific amounts, and tracked their progress diligently.

9.12 Emotional Aspects of Goal-Setting

Money goals can stir up various emotions—excitement, anxiety, hope, or even fear. Defining financial goals sometimes forces you to face the reality of your finances, which can be uncomfortable if you have more debt or less savings than you wish. Remember that it is normal to feel a bit uneasy when making big changes. The key is not to let negative emotions stop you.

Instead, channel your feelings into action. If you feel stressed about your debt level, let that stress motivate you to create a concrete plan to pay it down. If you are excited about retiring early, harness that excitement each time you are tempted to skip a contribution or overspend. Emotions can provide the energy you need to follow through on your plans—if you manage them wisely.

9.13 Accountability and Support Systems

Some people thrive on working toward goals privately, while others do better with external accountability. Consider whether you would benefit from:

- **A Financial Buddy**: A friend who also has goals. You can meet monthly to share updates.
- **Family Involvement**: If you are married or have children, get them on board so that everyone understands the family's financial targets.
- **Online Communities**: Many forums or social media groups exist for people paying off debt, saving aggressively, or pursuing early retirement. Sharing stories and tips can keep you motivated.
- **Professional Coaching**: A financial coach or counselor can give expert guidance and help you refine your goals.

What matters is having some form of support—human or digital—that encourages you to stay the course.

9.14 Visualizing Your Future Self

Sometimes, people lose motivation because the payoff for financial goals is far in the future. A helpful technique is to visualize or imagine your **future self** who has achieved the goal. What does your life look like after you clear that debt or save a down payment? How do you feel? What kinds of choices can you make now that were not possible before?

Detailed visualization can make long-term goals feel more real. You bridge the gap between today's efforts and tomorrow's rewards. This practice can also remind you that your daily choices have a direct impact on the quality of life your future self will experience.

9.15 Goal Overload and Burnout

While ambition is great, be cautious about setting too many major goals at once. Spreading yourself too thin can lead to feeling overwhelmed or even giving up when you cannot keep up with all your targets. It is often better to focus intensely on one or two critical goals and make steady progress, rather than half-heartedly juggle six or seven goals.

If you find yourself overwhelmed, list all your goals and prioritize them from most important to least important. Ask which ones can wait or can be scaled back. It is okay to tackle your biggest goals in phases. Slow, steady progress is still progress.

9.16 Goal-Tracking and Adjusting with Technology

Modern apps and tools can do more than just show you how much money you have saved. Some tools analyze your spending patterns, send you reminders when you are behind on your savings pace, or even suggest ways to cut costs so you can contribute more toward a goal. A few advanced apps use gamification—turning saving and investing into a game where you earn "badges" or "points" for achieving milestones.

If you enjoy technology, explore different platforms until you find one that resonates with you. However, if technology feels confusing or stressful, a simple pen-and-paper chart can still be very effective. The best system is the one you consistently use.

9.17 The Role of Mindset in Goal Achievement

We have talked about mindset a lot in earlier chapters. Here, it remains crucial. If you believe you cannot reach a goal, you will struggle to stay consistent. A "can-do" attitude, even if it feels forced at first, tends to lead to better outcomes. Replacing thoughts like "I'll never be able to save that much" with "I am learning how to save more each month" can shift your energy from defeat to possibility.

You might also consider positive affirmations or journaling about your progress. Write daily or weekly about what steps you took and how they bring you closer to your goal. This small habit can fortify your mindset against doubt or discouragement.

9.18 Handling Changes in Income

Many people experience changes in income—like getting a raise, changing jobs, losing a job, or picking up a side hustle. These shifts can either speed up your progress or slow it down:

- **Raises and Windfalls**: If you receive a raise at work, increase your monthly contributions to your goals before you get used to the extra money. That way, you do not inflate your lifestyle unnecessarily.
- **Job Loss**: If you lose a job, focus on essential expenses first and consider pausing non-urgent goals. Keep yourself afloat with your emergency fund if possible. Then, once you have a new job or income source, you can ramp up contributions again.
- **Side Hustles**: An additional source of income can be directed almost entirely to your financial goals. This approach can cut your goal timeline significantly.

Anticipate that life is not linear—income goes up and down, but your commitment to goals can remain steady by adjusting how you allocate funds in different seasons of life.

9.19 Celebrating Achievements

When you finally hit a major goal—like becoming debt-free or reaching your target down payment—take time to celebrate in a responsible way. You might do something fun that does not break the bank, such as a short weekend trip or a nice dinner at home with friends. Recognizing your hard work is crucial for preventing burnout and fueling you for the next big challenge.

Just ensure your celebration fits your budget. The point is to acknowledge your success, not to undo your progress by splurging recklessly.

9.20 Setting New Goals After Achieving Old Ones

Life does not stop once you meet your biggest goal. Often, people who finish paying off debt or buy a house realize they now have a new perspective and new ambitions. You might set a goal for early retirement, starting a business, or helping your kids fund their college education without taking massive loans. Financial growth is a journey—once you master one stage, you can take on bigger challenges.

9.21 Chapter Summary

1. **Goals Offer Direction**: Without goals, you risk drifting financially.
2. **Short-Term, Medium-Term, and Long-Term**: Each category keeps you motivated in different ways.
3. **S.M.A.R.T. Goals**: Specific, Measurable, Achievable, Relevant, Time-bound—use this framework to be precise.
4. **Tracking Methods**: Spreadsheets, apps, visuals—whatever keeps you consistent.
5. **Adjust When Needed**: Life changes, so your goals can change too.

9.22 Conclusion

Defining clear, meaningful financial goals is at the heart of purposeful money management. Whether you are saving for a dream vacation or planning for retirement, knowing where you want to go helps you map the journey. Tracking your progress, overcoming hurdles, and celebrating milestones along the way can turn your aspirations into reality. Remember, your goals do not just exist in your head—they are living markers of your future, guiding the choices you make every day.

CHAPTER 10: SMART SPENDING AND FRUGAL LIVING

10.1 Introduction: Changing How We Think About Spending

Living a frugal life does not mean you never enjoy yourself or buy nice things. It means you spend on what truly matters to you and skip or reduce spending on what does not. Frugality is about being smart with your money so you can channel more of it toward your goals—like saving, investing, or experiences that bring lasting value.

Many people mistake "frugal" for "cheap." But being frugal is not about refusing to spend a dime. It is about getting the most out of every dollar. Think of it as maximizing value while minimizing waste. Smart spending and frugal habits can free up resources to support your short-term and long-term financial goals.

10.2 The Mindset Behind Smart Spending

Your mindset plays a major role in how you spend money daily. If you believe you have to keep up with every new trend or gadget, you will likely overspend. If you think you "deserve" luxuries whenever you feel stressed, you might buy impulsively to soothe emotions. Smart spending involves a balance: you acknowledge your needs and desires, but you do not let them control your wallet.

Ask yourself before making a purchase:

1. **Do I really need this?**
2. **Does this align with my bigger goals or values?**
3. **Can I find a better price or a similar option at a discount?**
4. **Will I regret this purchase later?**

Pausing to reflect can reduce impulse buys and help you make more thoughtful decisions.

10.3 Tracking Your Spending Patterns

If you want to be a smarter spender, start by understanding **where** your money goes. Even if you have a budget, you may not realize how much you spend on small, day-to-day items—like coffee runs, snacks, or digital subscriptions. Try tracking every expense for at least a month. You can use a notebook, spreadsheet, or a budgeting app.

Look for patterns. Are you spending a lot on fast food because you skip meal planning? Are you paying for multiple streaming services you barely use? Identifying these "money leaks" is step one in living more frugally.

10.4 Separating Needs from Wants

A cornerstone of frugal living is distinguishing between needs and wants. **Needs** are expenses necessary for survival or well-being—like rent, groceries, utilities, and essential transportation. **Wants** are extras that can improve your lifestyle but are not strictly necessary—like dining out, entertainment, designer clothes, or the latest phone model.

This does not mean you should never buy wants, but it helps to prioritize. Maybe you value a gym membership because fitness is important, but you do not mind using a basic phone for a few years. Another person might skip the gym membership to save more, but spend on a nicer phone because they value tech. The trick is to align your spending with **your** values, not someone else's.

10.5 Budget-Friendly Shopping Strategies

Here are some practical ways to spend less without sacrificing quality:

1. **Price Comparisons**: Before buying an item, especially an expensive one, compare prices online and in different stores. A little research can save you a lot.
2. **Coupons and Discount Codes**: Use apps, newsletters, or coupon websites to find discounts on groceries, clothing, or household items.
3. **Buy Generic or Store Brands**: Often, store-brand products have the same ingredients as name brands but cost less.

4. **Shop Secondhand**: Thrift stores, consignment shops, or online marketplaces can be gold mines for clothing, furniture, and electronics at a fraction of their new cost.
5. **Buy in Bulk (If It Makes Sense)**: If you have the storage space and you use the product regularly, buying in bulk can lower the per-unit price. Just be careful not to buy items that expire quickly or that you will not really use.

10.6 Meal Planning and Eating at Home

Food often takes up a significant portion of a household budget. Frugal living often starts in the kitchen. If you eat out daily or buy lunches at work, costs add up quickly. Here are some tips:

- **Meal Planning**: Set aside time once a week to plan your meals. Write down a grocery list based on these meals so you only buy what you need.
- **Cook in Batches**: Prepare large meals you can freeze or eat over a couple of days, cutting down on cooking time and daily temptations to eat out.
- **Avoid Food Waste**: If you find yourself throwing out spoiled groceries, adjust your shopping. Buy less produce or freeze foods before they go bad.
- **Pack Lunches**: Bringing your lunch to work or school can save hundreds of dollars each month compared to buying fast food.
- **Limit Convenience Foods**: Pre-packaged meals or takeout might be handy, but they cost more than cooking from scratch.

These habits do more than save money; they can also lead to healthier eating if you choose nutritious ingredients.

10.7 The Art of Negotiation

Negotiation is not just for buying cars or houses. You can negotiate on many regular expenses—like phone bills, cable bills, insurance rates, or subscription services. Often, companies do not advertise lower prices, but if you call and politely ask for a discount or say you are considering switching to a competitor, they might offer a better deal.

You might feel uncomfortable negotiating at first, but there is little to lose. The worst they can say is "no." If they say "yes," you might lower your monthly bills significantly. Being polite but firm in stating your case—like mentioning you have a better offer from another provider—can be an effective approach.

10.8 Cutting Back on Impulse Purchases

Impulse buying is a major enemy of frugal living. You see a sale or something tempting, and you buy it without thinking. To fight this urge:

1. **Use a "Cooling-Off" Period**: Wait 24 hours (or even a week) before purchasing non-essential items. Often, the initial excitement fades, and you realize you do not need the item after all.
2. **Unsubscribe from Retail Emails**: Constant sale announcements can lure you into spending. Reduce these temptations by unsubscribing from store newsletters or turning off notifications.
3. **Avoid Mindless Browsing**: Do not surf online shopping sites when bored. This often leads to clicking "add to cart" without a real need.
4. **Leave Credit Cards at Home**: If you struggle with impulse buying in stores, bring only cash or a debit card. This physical limit can curb overspending.

10.9 Entertainment and Leisure on a Budget

Being frugal does not mean you can never have fun. It means finding cost-effective ways to enjoy life. Some ideas include:

- **Free Local Events**: Many communities offer free concerts, art shows, or outdoor festivals. Check local news or community boards.
- **Libraries**: Modern libraries often have more than just books. Some offer movie rentals, audiobooks, e-books, language courses, and even community events. All for free (or a very low membership cost).
- **Outdoor Activities**: Hiking, biking, picnics, and visiting local parks or beaches can be entertaining without high admission fees.
- **Game Nights**: Invite friends over for board games or potluck dinners. It is cheaper than going out and still very social.
- **Streaming Services**: If you love movies or TV shows, consider sharing streaming subscriptions with friends or family, or rotate which service you subscribe to each month.

Find creative ways to have a good time that do not require a big chunk of your paycheck. You might discover that simple pleasures are just as satisfying, if not more so, than expensive outings.

10.10 Transportation and Housing Hacks

Housing and transportation are usually among the largest expenses in anyone's budget. If you can reduce these costs, you free up money for other priorities:

- **Carpooling and Public Transport**: If you live in an area with decent public transportation, use it to save on gas, maintenance, and parking costs. Carpooling with coworkers can also help split expenses.
- **Buying a Reliable Used Car**: A brand-new car loses value the moment you drive it off the lot. A well-maintained used car can cost much less and still last for years.
- **Renting vs. Owning**: Depending on your city, renting may be cheaper in the short term, especially if housing prices are very high. Owning a home can be a good long-term investment, but also comes with property taxes, maintenance, and insurance. Decide based on your specific situation.
- **House Hacking**: If you own a property with extra space, consider renting out a room or turning the basement into a small apartment. The rental income can offset your mortgage or living costs.
- **Downsizing**: Some people choose a smaller living space or move to a cheaper neighborhood to significantly reduce monthly rent or mortgage payments.

10.11 Leveraging Technology for Deals

Besides using it to track your budget, technology can also help you save:

- **Price Comparison Websites**: Quickly check multiple vendors for the best price on a product.
- **Cashback and Reward Apps**: Some apps give you cash back or reward points when you shop at certain stores or buy specific products.
- **Alerts for Sales**: Set up price alerts that notify you when an item you want drops in price.
- **Online Coupon Codes**: Always check if a quick search for "[store name] coupon code" yields savings before finalizing an online purchase.

10.12 Repair and Reuse Mentality

A big part of frugal living is breaking the throwaway habit. Instead of discarding items as soon as they break or become slightly outdated, see if you can repair, repurpose, or upgrade them:

- **Clothing Repairs**: Learn basic sewing skills to patch holes or replace buttons.
- **DIY Home Fixes**: You can often handle simple repairs or maintenance tasks with help from online tutorials.
- **Upgrading Electronics**: Instead of buying a new laptop, sometimes adding more RAM or a new hard drive can extend its life.
- **Refinish or Repaint Furniture**: A coat of paint or some new upholstery can transform an old piece into something fresh.

Not only does this mindset save money, but it also reduces waste and is better for the environment.

10.13 Building a Capsule Wardrobe

For those who love fashion but want to stay frugal, consider a **capsule wardrobe**. This involves owning fewer, high-quality clothes that all work well together. The idea is to have a mix of basic, versatile items that you can combine in many ways. This reduces the desire to keep buying new outfits, because you always have multiple looks from the core pieces you own. Quality over quantity becomes the guiding principle. You might spend a bit more on each item, but buy fewer items overall, which can save money in the long run.

10.14 Handling Peer Pressure

One challenge to staying frugal is dealing with friends or family who want to eat out often, go on expensive outings, or buy fancy stuff. You might worry that people will judge you if you say "no" or suggest cheaper alternatives.

Try these approaches:

1. **Explain Your Why**: If they are close friends, share that you are working toward a specific financial goal, like buying a house or clearing debt. Some might support you more than you expect.

2. **Offer Alternatives**: Suggest a potluck, a movie night at home, or a hike instead of an expensive restaurant. You do not have to eliminate socializing; just change how it looks.
3. **Budget for Social Events**: If you truly want to join an occasional outing, set aside a small "fun fund" each month. This way, you do not feel guilty or go off track when you do decide to spend money with friends.
4. **Stand Firm**: Ultimately, your financial well-being is more important than impressing others. True friends will respect your choices.

10.15 Financial Minimalism

Financial minimalism is an approach where you intentionally reduce unnecessary complexity and clutter in your finances. This might mean:

- Having fewer bank accounts or credit cards so it is easier to track spending.
- Minimizing subscription services to only what you regularly use.
- Simplifying your investment choices (for example, using diversified index funds rather than juggling dozens of stocks).
- Keeping your material possessions at a level that matches your needs and genuinely brings you joy.

By adopting financial minimalism, you may find you have less stress and fewer expenses, freeing up resources for what matters most.

10.16 The Mental and Emotional Benefits of Frugality

There is more to frugal living than just saving money. Many people find that reducing unnecessary spending and clutter in their lives reduces stress. They worry less about credit card bills or whether they are living beyond their means. Simpler choices can also free up mental energy.

When you live frugally, you become more intentional and grateful for what you have. You see money as a tool to achieve important goals, rather than a means to buy happiness. That shift can bring a sense of peace and control over your life, which is priceless.

10.17 Teaching Frugal Habits to Children

If you have kids, you can set them up for lifelong success by demonstrating and explaining frugal habits:

- **Involve Them in Meal Planning**: Let them pick recipes and help with a grocery list. Show them how to compare prices.
- **Give Them an Allowance**: Let them learn by managing a small sum. If they spend it all on candy, they learn the consequence of not having money for a toy they want later.
- **Encourage Saving**: Help them set a goal, like saving for a special toy, and match some of their savings (like a mini "employer match").
- **Explain the Reasoning**: Kids might ask, "Why don't we buy that brand-new gadget?" Instead of just saying "we can't afford it," talk about how money spent here means less for other things (like family vacations or sports activities).

Over time, they will absorb the idea that money is finite and that wise choices make a big difference.

10.18 Balancing Frugality with Enjoyment

Frugality should not make you miserable. If you truly love lattes, build a small coffee budget. If you find deep happiness in traveling, save up for trips in a strategic, cost-effective way rather than saying no to travel forever. The goal is to cut back on wasteful or mindless spending so you can afford what really adds value to your life.

Try adopting a "spend extravagantly on what you love, cut ruthlessly on what you don't" mindset. That means you do not waste money on things that do not matter to you, leaving more resources to fund the few items or experiences that do matter.

10.19 Dealing with Setbacks in Frugal Living

Just like any lifestyle change, frugal living can face hiccups. You might slip into old habits or get hit with an unexpected bill that forces you to spend more than planned. Treat these moments as lessons. Ask:

- **Why did this slip-up happen?**

- How can I prepare better next time?
- Do I need to adjust my budget or my spending triggers?

Forgive yourself, learn from the mistake, and get back on track. Building frugal habits is a process, not a sprint.

10.20 Real-Life Examples of Smart Spenders

Case Study 1: Nolan and Grocery Savings

Nolan realized he was spending $500 a month on groceries and $200 on takeout. He began meal planning every Sunday, cutting his grocery bill to $300. By cooking large batches, he drastically reduced takeout. He saved $400 a month total and put that into an emergency fund. Over a year, that is $4,800—enough to handle unexpected car repairs or take a modest vacation.

Case Study 2: Alice's Entertainment Budget

Alice loved movies and restaurants. She used to spend $200 a month on movie tickets and $300 on dining out. After seeing how this hurt her savings, she invited friends over for potlucks and movie nights at home. She kept one or two dinners out per month as a treat. Her new entertainment spending dropped to $150 a month. That $350 a month difference now goes into her "home renovation fund," and she says she actually enjoys socializing more because it is more personal and fun at home.

10.21 Chapter Summary

1. **Frugal Living Is About Value**: It is not about depriving yourself but optimizing where your money goes.
2. **Needs vs. Wants**: Prioritize what truly matters and cut back on what doesn't.
3. **Practical Tips**: Meal planning, negotiation, buying secondhand, using discounts, and adopting a repair-and-reuse mindset can save big.
4. **Emotional Benefits**: Less financial stress, greater appreciation for what you have, and more freedom to fund meaningful goals.
5. **Balance Is Key**: You do not have to say "no" to everything; spend on what brings real joy and cut the rest.

10.22 Conclusion

Smart spending and frugal living are powerful ways to protect your finances while still enjoying life. By becoming more aware of how and why you spend, you can eliminate wasteful habits, prioritize the things you care about most, and accelerate your progress toward important financial goals. This chapter wraps up the core idea that money is a resource—it works best when spent with intention and thoughtfulness.

CHAPTER 11: INCREASING YOUR INCOME WITH SIDE HUSTLES AND MORE

11.1 Why Increasing Your Income Matters

By now, you have learned about saving money, handling debt, setting goals, and living frugally. These steps are essential for a strong financial foundation. Yet, there is another key factor that can speed up your progress: **increasing your income**. When you have more money coming in, you can save more, invest more, pay off debt faster, and even afford some of the things you love without jeopardizing your future.

Relying on just one source of income can sometimes be risky. If something goes wrong with your main job—like a sudden layoff or a business closure—you might struggle to cover your bills. Having extra sources of income not only boosts your financial security but can also help you reach your goals sooner. The good news is that today's world offers many ways to earn more, from freelance work and online platforms to creating a small business on the side.

11.2 Understanding Your Current Skill Set

Before diving into new opportunities, it is helpful to analyze your current skills. Everyone has something they are good at or enjoy doing. Perhaps you speak more than one language, have artistic talent, or excel at organizing and planning. Even if you think your skills are ordinary, there may be a market for them. For instance, are you good with children, animals, or computers? Can you write or design? Are you a skilled craftsman or handy around the house?

Make a list of activities you do well or hobbies you enjoy. From there, consider which of those might be turned into a source of income. Sometimes, what seems like a small skill—like writing short stories—could grow into a profitable side hustle if you dig deeper into the possibilities. Or maybe your knack for photography can help you sell pictures online. By identifying your skills, you can start to see which income avenues make the most sense for you.

11.3 Exploring Different Side Hustle Ideas

In today's economy, the term "side hustle" simply refers to any kind of work you do to earn extra money besides your main job or role. The range of side hustles is huge, and there is likely an option that fits your lifestyle and talents. Below are some popular categories:

1. **Freelancing**: If you have a skill like writing, graphic design, programming, video editing, or coaching, you can offer your services to clients. Many websites help freelancers connect with businesses or individuals who need specific tasks done.
2. **Tutoring and Teaching**: Are you good at math, music, or a foreign language? You can tutor students—either in person or online. Some people even teach classes on topics like cooking or painting through local community centers or digital platforms.
3. **Selling Products Online**: Platforms exist for almost anything you want to sell—like handmade crafts, digital art, vintage clothing, or even your own e-books. You can also explore dropshipping (selling products shipped directly from a supplier) if you prefer not to store inventory.
4. **Gig Economy Work**: Services such as ride-sharing, food delivery, dog walking, and package courier options let you earn money in a flexible schedule. You can also find tasks like assembling furniture or doing yard work for neighbors through local apps or community boards.
5. **House-Sitting or Pet-Sitting**: If you have extra time, you can watch people's homes or pets when they travel. Some positions may be short-term, while others could last weeks. This is especially viable if you live in an area with frequent travelers.
6. **Content Creation**: Some people earn money by creating engaging content on social media platforms—like YouTube, TikTok, or Instagram. If you have a knack for entertaining or educating an audience, you can monetize through ads, sponsorships, or brand deals. This path can take time to build but can become lucrative if your channel grows.

These are just starting points. Look at your list of skills and see if any side hustle aligns well. A good side job should be something you can manage alongside your primary work or responsibilities without burning out too quickly.

11.4 Balancing Your Main Job with a Side Hustle

When starting a new income stream, time management is crucial. You might have a full-time job, family commitments, or other responsibilities. Adding extra work to your schedule can be challenging. Here are some tips for balance:

1. **Set Realistic Hours**: Decide how many hours per week you can comfortably devote to the side hustle. Maybe that is 5 hours on weekends or 2 hours each evening. Stick to it so you do not burn out.
2. **Plan Carefully**: Use a calendar to map out deadlines or project milestones. Include your main job's schedule, family events, and personal downtime. The more structured you are, the easier it is to stay on top of everything.
3. **Delegate or Simplify**: If your side hustle becomes more demanding, see if you can simplify tasks at home—like meal prepping for the week or asking family members to share chores. Small changes can free up more time.
4. **Take Breaks**: Overworking can lead to stress or even health problems. Make sure you have at least one day a week where you slow down, rest, or enjoy leisure activities. Striking a healthy work-life balance is key to long-term success in both your main job and your side hustle.

11.5 How to Price Your Services or Products

One tricky part of earning extra money is figuring out what to charge. Price too high, and you might struggle to find customers. Price too low, and you could be selling yourself short. Here are some strategies:

1. **Research the Market**: Look at what others with similar skills or products charge. This gives you a baseline.
2. **Consider Your Experience**: If you are brand-new, you might start on the lower side to build a portfolio or get testimonials. If you are experienced, do not be shy about setting a rate that reflects your value.
3. **Factor in Costs**: If your side hustle involves materials, shipping, software subscriptions, or travel, include those costs in your pricing. Otherwise, you could end up making little profit.
4. **Keep Testing**: Try one price and see how the market responds. If you are swamped with orders, you might be too cheap. If you are getting very few clients, consider adjusting or adding more value to your offer (like extra features or perks).

Remember to track your expenses and income so you know exactly how much you are making after costs. Your goal is to earn a profit, not just extra busywork.

11.6 Negotiating a Raise at Your Main Job

Sometimes, the easiest way to increase your income is right where you already work. If you have been a loyal, productive employee, you might have room to negotiate a raise or promotion. Here are some tips:

1. **Track Your Achievements**: Keep a record of your contributions—like projects you completed, money you saved the company, or clients you brought in. Having clear evidence of your value makes your case stronger.
2. **Know Your Market Value**: Check job postings or salary comparison websites to see what others in your position typically earn. If you find you are earning less than the market rate, that is useful information to bring up during discussions.
3. **Prepare for the Conversation**: Schedule a meeting with your manager or supervisor. Be professional and factual. Explain why you deserve a raise, focusing on your contributions and the value you add.
4. **Offer Solutions**: Sometimes, companies have budget constraints. If so, suggest alternatives—like more flexible hours, extra training, or a plan to review your compensation again in a few months after you hit specific targets.

If you cannot get a raise now, do not be discouraged. Ask what steps or performance goals you need to meet to earn one in the future. That clarity can help you focus your efforts.

11.7 Developing In-Demand Skills

If your current skill set does not easily lend itself to a side hustle, consider building **new** skills that the market rewards. In the digital age, there are countless ways to learn—from online tutorials and courses to local classes or mentorship programs. Skills that can lead to higher income might include:

1. **Coding or Web Development**: The demand for websites, apps, and online services is still huge. Even basic coding skills can open doors to freelance work or higher-paying jobs.

2. **Digital Marketing and Social Media Management**: Small businesses need help reaching customers online. Learning how to run social media campaigns, analyze website traffic, or manage email lists can make you valuable.
3. **Writing and Content Creation**: Companies need blog posts, press releases, and newsletters. Polishing your writing skills can lead to freelance gigs or full-time offers.
4. **Graphic Design and Video Editing**: Visual content is always in demand—especially for online ads, social media, and corporate materials.
5. **Specialized Services**: This could include bookkeeping, life coaching, event planning, or even 3D printing if you have the equipment. Look for niches with consistent demand but not too much competition.

Learning a new skill might take time and sometimes money for courses, but it can drastically improve your earning potential. Think of it as an investment in yourself. The higher your skill level, the more you can charge or the better your chances of landing a higher-paying job.

11.8 Turning Hobbies into Income

Sometimes, a hobby can evolve into a small (or even significant) business. This path can be especially fulfilling because you are doing something you already enjoy. For example:

- **Gardening**: If you love growing plants or vegetables, you might sell herbs, seedlings, or produce at local markets.
- **Baking or Cooking**: If people rave about your pastries or unique dishes, consider catering small events or selling specialty items online.
- **Crafts and Art**: Handmade jewelry, pottery, custom paintings—these can find an audience at craft fairs or through online shops.
- **Music**: If you play an instrument, you could teach beginners or perform at local venues.
- **Fitness**: Love working out? Train for a fitness certification and offer personal training or small group classes in your free time.

Be cautious not to let the pressure of making money ruin the joy you get from the hobby. Start small, set fair prices, and see if the demand is there. If it grows, fantastic. If not, you still have the hobby you love.

11.9 Networking for Opportunities

Whether you want a side hustle or a better position at your main job, **networking** can open many doors. You do not have to be an outgoing extrovert to build connections. Start by:

1. **Attending Events**: Look for local meetups, industry conferences, or community gatherings that match your interests or career. Talk to people and share what you do.
2. **Using Social Media**: Platforms like LinkedIn are designed for professional networking. You can also find niche Facebook groups or Discord servers related to your skill or side hustle.
3. **Helping Others**: Offer small favors or advice when possible. Networking is not just about taking—it is about mutual support. People remember those who help them, and they may return the favor later.

A strong network might introduce you to new clients, tell you about a job opening before it is posted publicly, or mentor you in a skill you are developing.

11.10 Managing Taxes and Financial Records

As you start earning more, you will need to keep track of your income and expenses for tax purposes. Ignoring this can lead to headaches later. Basic steps include:

- **Separate Your Finances**: If possible, open a separate bank account for your side hustle income and related expenses. This makes it easier to track.
- **Keep Receipts and Invoices**: A simple spreadsheet or accounting software can help record what you earn and what you spend.
- **Learn Local Tax Rules**: Depending on where you live, you may need to file quarterly tax payments if you earn a certain amount outside your regular job. Check government websites or consult a tax professional for accurate guidance.
- **Consider Deductions**: If you work from home on your side hustle, some expenses—like part of your internet bill—may be deductible. Again, ask a qualified professional if you are unsure.

Being organized keeps you out of trouble and helps you see whether your side hustle is truly profitable. It also saves you from scrambling to find documents during tax season.

11.11 Knowing When to Scale Up (or Step Back)

Not every side hustle is meant to become a full-blown business, and that is okay. For some people, a modest extra $200 a month is enough to meet certain goals. Others see their small venture grow to the point where they consider going full-time. If you reach a point where demand for your product or service is high and you are making significant money, you might choose to quit your main job to focus on the new enterprise.

On the other hand, you may find your side hustle becomes too stressful or interferes with other parts of your life. If that happens, stepping back or pausing is perfectly valid. The key is to stay in tune with your goals and overall well-being. Do not let the pursuit of extra income derail your health or relationships.

11.12 Creating Multiple Streams of Income

Increasing your income does not have to come from just one source. Many people adopt a **multiple streams of income** approach—like a main job, one or two side hustles, and perhaps passive income through investments. Diversifying your income can provide a cushion if one stream experiences a downturn. For example, if you are a teacher, you might also tutor online and sell lesson plans on a digital marketplace, plus invest part of your earnings for dividends or interest.

This approach must be managed carefully. Too many projects at once might cause burnout. But if you can handle your schedule wisely, multiple streams of income can help you reach financial stability faster.

11.13 Time vs. Money: Finding the Right Balance

Yes, making more money is beneficial. However, it is also important to remember that your time is a limited resource. You cannot work every hour of the day. And even if you could, you might harm your mental and physical health. That is why it is essential to strike a balance between earning and living a fulfilling life.

Ask yourself:

1. **What Are My Primary Goals?** If you are trying to pay off debt quickly or build a down payment for a house, maybe you will push yourself harder for a year or two.
2. **What About Hobbies and Family Time?** If your side hustle is eroding family dinners or personal hobbies you love, reconsider how many hours you devote to it.
3. **Can I Work Smarter?** Maybe there is a more efficient way to earn money—like automating parts of your process, delegating tasks, or focusing on higher-paying jobs rather than many small ones.

In the end, the ideal scenario is one in which you steadily increase your income while still enjoying life. Money should be a tool, not a chain around your neck.

11.14 Chapter Summary

1. **Boosting Income = Faster Progress**: More income allows you to save more, pay off debt, and invest.
2. **Side Hustles Are Diverse**: From freelancing and gig economy jobs to selling crafts online, there is likely an option for your skill set.
3. **Balance and Strategy**: Manage your time wisely, set fair prices, and keep financial records.
4. **Consider a Raise or New Skills**: Sometimes the simplest path is negotiating a raise or learning a high-demand skill.
5. **Keep Health and Happiness in Mind**: Extra money is great, but do not sacrifice your well-being in the process.

11.15 Conclusion

Increasing your income can accelerate your path to financial freedom, but it requires planning, effort, and mindful decision-making. Whether you find extra work through a side hustle, negotiate a better salary, or transform a hobby into a profitable venture, the steps you take should align with your broader financial goals and personal values. As you move forward, remember to maintain a healthy balance and stay organized, so your pursuit of more income remains a positive addition to your life.

CHAPTER 12: THE IMPORTANCE OF PERSISTENCE AND DISCIPLINE

12.1 Defining Persistence and Discipline

All your financial knowledge—managing money, paying off debt, saving, investing, and even boosting your income—relies on two powerful qualities: **persistence** (the ability to keep going despite challenges) and **discipline** (the ability to stick to a plan, even when it is not convenient).

- **Persistence** is about not giving up, whether you face unexpected medical bills, job uncertainty, or a drop in investment values. When setbacks arise, persistent people find solutions, learn from mistakes, and continue moving forward.
- **Discipline** involves making the right choices consistently over time. It is turning down an expensive impulse buy because it does not align with your goals. It is putting money into savings each month, even when you would rather spend it on fun things. Discipline makes habits strong; persistence keeps you from quitting.

12.2 Why These Traits Are Crucial in Personal Finance

Money management is not a one-time action; it is a lifelong journey. You do not just save once, budget once, or invest once—you do these things repeatedly, often for years or even decades. That is where discipline comes in. If you only follow a budget for one month and then abandon it, you lose the benefit. If you only save sporadically, your emergency fund or future nest egg might not grow as needed.

Likewise, persistence is necessary because financial challenges are common. You may face job loss, market downturns, family emergencies, or temptations to overspend. Without persistence, you might lose sight of your goals at the first sign of trouble. In contrast, persistent individuals adapt their plans or timelines but keep chasing the same end result.

12.3 Common Obstacles to Staying Disciplined

Many distractions and temptations can derail your financial plan. Here are a few common ones:

1. **Impulse Buying**: Retailers and online shops are masters of making purchases feel urgent or necessary. Flash sales, limited-time offers, and "buy-now-pay-later" options lure you in.
2. **Lifestyle Creep**: When your income goes up, it is easy to spend more on unnecessary luxuries, quickly wiping out any extra financial benefit.
3. **Peer Pressure**: Friends and family can unintentionally (or intentionally) push you to spend. If everyone else is upgrading cars or going on expensive vacations, you might feel left out.
4. **Emotional Spending**: Stress, boredom, or sadness can lead people to "comfort buy." While it may feel good temporarily, it often hurts your financial situation in the long run.

Recognizing these triggers helps you plan how to deal with them. For example, you might unsubscribe from marketing emails or plan a small "fun fund" so you do not go overboard when you feel the urge to spend.

12.4 Strategies for Building Persistence

Persistence is like a muscle—you strengthen it over time. Here are ways to build it:

1. **Set Clear, Meaningful Goals**: The more a goal matters to you emotionally, the harder you will fight to achieve it. Remind yourself regularly of the "why" behind your financial plan.
2. **Break Big Tasks into Smaller Steps**: Large goals can seem intimidating. Splitting them into small, achievable tasks makes them feel more doable. Each small success fuels your persistence.
3. **Embrace a Learning Mindset**: Treat every setback as a lesson. If you blow your budget one month, ask what went wrong. Use that information to do better next month.
4. **Develop a Support System**: Friends, family, online groups, or a mentor can motivate you when you feel like quitting. Simply talking about your struggles can reignite your determination.

5. **Celebrate Milestones**: Persistence gets easier when you acknowledge progress. If you paid off a credit card or saved your first $1,000, reward yourself (modestly) and appreciate how far you have come.

12.5 Building Discipline Through Habits and Routines

Discipline often depends on setting up routines that make good choices easier and bad choices harder. Some practical tips:

1. **Automate Good Behaviors**: Set up automatic transfers to savings or investments. If the money never hits your checking account, you are less tempted to spend it.
2. **Create a Consistent Budget Schedule**: Choose a specific day each week or month to review your budget and finances. This regular check-in keeps you aware of your progress and any issues.
3. **Limit Access to Temptations**: If impulse buying is a problem, remove your stored credit card details from online shops, unsubscribe from sale alerts, and maybe keep your credit card in a drawer instead of your wallet.
4. **Track Your Choices**: Use a habit tracker for specific financial behaviors—like "did I stick to my meal plan this week?" or "did I log every purchase?" Seeing checkmarks grow can be motivating.
5. **Plan for Treats**: Discipline does not mean zero fun. Allocate some money each month for small indulgences. Knowing you can spend guilt-free on something you love keeps you from feeling deprived.

12.6 Overcoming Plateaus and Boredom

It is normal to feel excited when you first create a budget or start a saving plan, but that excitement may fade over time. Eventually, you might reach a plateau or feel bored with the slow progress. How can you push through?

- **Revisit Your Goals**: Sometimes writing them down again or creating a fresh vision board sparks renewed interest.
- **Try a New Challenge**: For instance, do a "no-spend weekend" or a month where you aim to reduce grocery bills by 10%. Challenges can make routine tasks feel exciting.
- **Change Your Approach**: If you have always tracked finances on paper, try an app (or vice versa). A new tool can freshen up the process.

- **Study Success Stories**: Read about people who overcame bigger obstacles. Their stories might inspire you to keep going.

Plateaus are natural, but they do not have to end your journey. Viewing them as a normal phase of growth helps you stay patient.

12.7 The Role of Mindset in Persistence and Discipline

We have often talked about mindset throughout this book for a good reason. What you believe about yourself and your future influences how you handle challenges. For example:

- **Fixed Mindset**: "I am bad at saving. I will never be able to retire comfortably."
- **Growth Mindset**: "I can learn better money habits. If I keep trying, I will improve over time."

When you have a growth mindset, setbacks become learning opportunities. You see effort and discipline as paths to growth, not burdens. This viewpoint nurtures persistence because you believe your actions can change outcomes.

12.8 Dealing with Setbacks and Failures

Let us be honest: almost everyone faces financial bumps. Maybe you lose a job, take on unexpected medical debt, or watch your investments dip. Discipline and persistence shine brightest during these storms. How to cope:

1. **Assess the Damage**: First, understand how serious the setback is. Can you cover it with your emergency fund? Do you need a short-term loan? The clearer the picture, the better you can respond.
2. **Adapt Your Plan**: You might need to reduce retirement contributions for a bit, pause extra debt payments, or find a short-term side hustle to fill the gap. Adjusting your plan is better than abandoning it.
3. **Stay Calm**: Panic often leads to poor decisions. Take a breath, talk to someone you trust, and think logically about the next steps.
4. **Rebuild and Learn**: Once you stabilize, figure out what could prevent a similar crisis in the future—maybe a bigger emergency fund, better insurance, or updating your skills to be more employable.

Failures do not define you unless you stop trying altogether. Even if you have to start from scratch, discipline and persistence can guide you back onto the path.

12.9 Finding Inspiration in Role Models

Look at people who have achieved the financial goals you desire—like someone who paid off $100,000 in student loans or built a thriving business from scratch. Reading or listening to their stories can provide:

- **Practical Tips**: You can learn new techniques or strategies they used.
- **Motivation**: Seeing that an ordinary person overcame big obstacles can help you believe you can do the same.
- **Accountability**: Role models remind you what is possible. If they did it, why not you?

Role models can be famous authors, local community members, or even online acquaintances in personal finance forums. Absorb their insights and adapt them to your situation.

12.10 Accountability Partners and Support Systems

Working on financial goals alone can be tough. Many people find it easier to persist when they have someone who checks in on them. This could be a friend with similar goals, a family member who supports you, or even an online group. You can share:

- **Weekly Progress**: "I saved $50 this week toward my car fund."
- **Challenges**: "I struggled not to eat out. Need tips!"
- **Ideas and Resources**: "Found a great budgeting app!"
- **Celebrations**: "I just hit $1,000 in my emergency fund!"

Knowing someone will ask about your progress can push you to maintain discipline. You also get emotional support when you feel discouraged.

12.11 Using Visual Reminders

A simple way to keep discipline strong is by placing visual reminders of your goals where you see them every day. It could be:

- **A Picture**: Maybe an image of a dream house, a vacation spot, or something symbolizing financial freedom.
- **A Thermometer Chart**: Color in the amount of debt paid off or savings reached.
- **Post-It Notes**: Write your main goal on a sticky note and put it on your computer or bathroom mirror.

These small cues can jolt you out of autopilot spending or remind you why you are skipping that extra online shopping spree. It might seem trivial, but consistent nudges can have a real impact on your day-to-day choices.

12.12 Discipline Over Willpower

People sometimes say they rely on "willpower" to resist spending. But willpower alone can be tricky because it fluctuates with your mood, energy levels, or stress. A better approach is to set systems and rules that reduce the need for willpower. For instance:

- **Automatic Transfers**: If you know you want to save $300 a month, automate it. You do not have to decide each time or fight the temptation to spend that money instead.
- **Cash-Only Policy**: If you overspend with credit cards, limit yourself to cash for non-bill items. Once the cash is gone, it is gone.
- **Limited Shopping Hours**: If online shopping is your weakness, maybe you decide you can only browse or buy once a week for a set time.

The fewer choices you leave to emotional "in-the-moment" willpower, the more consistent you become. This is discipline at work—setting up frameworks that guide your behavior.

12.13 Compounding Benefits of Persistence and Discipline

Just like money can compound over time (Chapter 8), so can your good habits. Each time you resist an unnecessary purchase, you not only save money but also strengthen your self-control for the next challenge. Each success feeds another. Over months and years, disciplined behaviors can become second nature. The effect compounds in the form of growing savings, decreasing debt, and increased confidence in handling money.

Conversely, giving up at the first hiccup can form negative habits—like turning to credit cards whenever life gets tough. Recognizing that discipline has a snowball effect helps you power through the initial difficulties.

12.14 Practical Exercises to Boost Financial Discipline

You can practice discipline like any skill. Try these exercises:

1. **No-Spend Challenges**: For a set period—like a week or month—commit to not buying anything beyond absolute essentials (groceries, bills, etc.). Keep track of how it feels and how much you save.
2. **Delayed Gratification**: If you want something non-essential, write it down on a "wish list" with the date. If you still want it 30 days later and it fits your budget, then buy it. Often, you lose interest before the 30 days are up.
3. **Budget Hurdle**: Aim to reduce one large expense category by a certain percentage for a month—maybe groceries or entertainment—just to see if you can. This trains you to spot savings you did not think were possible.
4. **Tracking Challenges**: Keep a notebook or a notes app on your phone and jot down every expense for two weeks straight. This heightened awareness can make you more thoughtful about spending.

Each of these exercises forces you to confront habits and develop your "discipline muscle."

12.15 Linking Financial Habits to Your Personal Identity

When you start seeing yourself as someone who is disciplined and persistent, money habits become part of who you are, not just tasks on a list. Telling yourself, "I am someone who plans ahead and saves," can shift your actions. Aligning money habits with your identity makes them more natural to maintain because breaking them would feel like breaking your own character.

For instance, if a friend suggests an expensive outing you cannot afford, you might respond: "I'm careful about my spending because I'm saving for my dream trip." You frame it as part of who you are, not just an external rule you are forced to follow.

12.16 Stories of Persistence and Discipline in Money

Case Study 1: Raul's Debt Snowball
Raul had multiple credit cards and a personal loan adding up to $25,000. At first, he felt overwhelmed. But he used a snowball method to tackle them one by one, starting with the smallest balance to build momentum. He faced unexpected car repairs and a minor medical bill during the process, but persisted by cutting back on dining out and even picking up a weekend job. After 18 months, he cleared all debts. Raul credits his daily habit of tracking expenses and a weekly budget review with keeping him disciplined.

Case Study 2: Jasmine's Investing Routine
Jasmine, 25, decided she wanted to retire by 50. She automatically invested 15% of her salary every month into index funds, no matter what. When the market dipped, her family urged her to stop investing. She persevered, continuing to buy shares at lower prices. Over the next decade, her portfolio grew significantly. She calls her routine "paying future Jasmine," and it keeps her disciplined during both good and bad market times.

12.17 Checking In with Yourself Regularly

Your finances are not static, and neither are your motivations. Regular self-checks can help you stay disciplined:

1. **Monthly Reflection**: Ask, "Did I stick to my budget? Where did I struggle? What can I improve next month?"
2. **Quarterly Goal Review**: Look at your savings, investments, and debt reduction every three months. Are you on track to hit your bigger goals for the year?
3. **Yearly Life Audit**: Once a year, go deeper. Are you satisfied with your job, your side hustle, your progress toward buying a house, or your retirement timeline? This bigger picture check can reignite your passion or prompt you to make key adjustments.

12.18 Rewarding Yourself the Smart Way

Persisting and staying disciplined does not mean depriving yourself forever. Incorporate **planned** rewards that will not sabotage your finances. This could be:

- A small percentage of any windfall (like a bonus) toward a fun activity.
- A modest celebration each time you reach a key milestone—like paying off a credit card in full.
- Upgrading one item in your life that you use daily and truly appreciate, like a better desk chair if you work from home, or better cooking tools if you love to cook.

The secret is that the reward is part of the plan, not an impulse decision that undermines your goals.

12.19 The Long-Term Payoff

Why push yourself to be disciplined and persistent? Because over time, these traits can lead to:

- **Financial Security**: An ample emergency fund, minimal debt, and growing investments.
- **Freedom to Choose**: You might shift careers, start a business, or retire earlier, knowing you have a financial cushion.
- **Peace of Mind**: Less money stress, better sleep, and improved relationships due to fewer financial conflicts.
- **Opportunity**: When you have your finances in order, you can jump on opportunities—like investing in a promising startup or taking a career risk—because you have the safety net and mindset to handle it.

These benefits often snowball. The discipline you show in one area of your life can spill over into other areas—like your health, family routines, or career growth. It is a cycle of continuous self-improvement.

12.20 Chapter Summary

1. **Persistence and Discipline Are the Glue**: They hold your financial plans together over time.
2. **Obstacles Are Normal**: Expect them—impulse buys, emergencies, and emotional spending—but plan for how to handle them.
3. **Habits and Routines Help**: By automating good behaviors and reducing temptations, you rely less on sheer willpower.
4. **Mindset Matters**: A growth mindset sees setbacks as lessons, not reasons to quit.

5. **Rewards and Flexibility**: Maintain discipline long-term by allowing planned treats and adjusting goals as life changes.

12.21 Conclusion

Persistence and discipline form the backbone of successful money management. They are what keep you saving, investing, budgeting, and earning more, month after month and year after year. Life will test your resolve, but the ability to stay on track—adjusting plans as needed—ultimately brings you closer to your greatest financial hopes. Whether you are striving to get out of debt, buy a house, travel the world, or retire early, these two traits can guide you past the inevitable bumps on the road to financial freedom.

CHAPTER 13: MASTERING NEGOTIATION AND GETTING GOOD DEALS

13.1 Introduction: The Power of Negotiation

Negotiation is a skill that helps you get better value for your money. It can lower the prices you pay for products or services, or increase what you earn for your time and skills. In other words, negotiation helps you spend less and earn more—two key elements in a healthy financial life. Often, we think of negotiation as something that happens only in boardrooms or when buying a house or car. The reality is that negotiation can happen in daily life—like asking for a discount on a slightly damaged item in a store, requesting a lower interest rate from a lender, or discussing a salary raise at work.

Mastering negotiation does not mean you have to be pushy or aggressive. It involves knowing your worth, doing research, and communicating well. Many people feel nervous about negotiating, but once you learn a few strategies, you will see that negotiation is not about "winning" at someone else's expense. Instead, it is about finding a fair outcome where both sides feel satisfied. By being polite, informed, and confident, you can often get better deals in many parts of your life.

13.2 Changing Your Mindset About Negotiation

One of the first steps in becoming a better negotiator is recognizing that negotiation is normal and acceptable. Some people skip negotiating because they do not want to seem rude. Others worry they will be turned down. But in many cultures and situations, negotiation is simply part of the process. Retailers may mark up their products expecting that some people will haggle. Employers know that job candidates may negotiate salary or benefits.

Changing your mindset means understanding that asking for a better deal is not selfish or impolite, as long as you are respectful. It is a conversation. You are not making demands; you are discussing terms. If the other party can offer something better—like a lower price or an added benefit—they will let you know. If not, you can either accept their final offer or walk away. The key is that you have nothing to lose by trying, and you may gain a lot.

13.3 Preparing for a Negotiation

Good negotiators do not walk into a conversation unprepared. They gather facts, outline their goals, and plan for possible outcomes. Here are some steps to prepare:

1. **Research**: Find out the usual price of the product or service you want, or the market salary for your position. Look at different stores or job listings to understand typical rates. This knowledge helps you avoid overpaying or underselling yourself.
2. **Set Your Target**: Decide the ideal outcome you would like. For example, if you are buying a used car, what is the highest price you are willing to pay? If you are negotiating salary, what figure do you aim for?
3. **Know Your Walk-Away Point**: This is the maximum (or minimum) you will accept before you walk away. If the other side cannot meet your limit, you should be ready to leave.
4. **Consider Possible Benefits or Extras**: Sometimes, you can negotiate more than just price. For a car purchase, you might ask for free maintenance or an extended warranty. For a salary negotiation, you could request extra vacation days or a flexible schedule if the employer cannot budge on base pay.
5. **Plan Your Approach**: Decide how you will open the conversation, what reasons you will give for requesting a better deal, and how you will respond if you get pushback. Having a strategy reduces nervousness and confusion during the actual talk.

13.4 Basic Negotiation Strategies

You do not need fancy tactics to negotiate effectively. Some simple but powerful approaches include:

1. **Polite Yet Firm**: Be friendly and courteous, but stand your ground. It is okay to say, "I appreciate your offer, but can we talk about improving this price (or salary)?"
2. **Silence Is Golden**: After you make a request—like a lower price or a higher wage—pause. Silence can be uncomfortable, and sometimes the other person will fill it by meeting your terms or improving the offer.
3. **Focus on Value, Not Just Price**: You can say things like, "I like the product, but at this cost, it is not quite worth it to me. Can we discuss a

price that makes sense for both of us?" This shows you respect the seller's need to profit, but you also want a fair deal.
4. **Ask Open-Ended Questions**: Instead of asking "Is that your lowest price?" you can ask, "How flexible are you on the price?" or "What else can you include to make this deal more appealing?" Open-ended questions invite discussion.
5. **Package Deals**: If you are buying multiple items or have several aspects to negotiate, bundle them together. For instance, if you are negotiating with a contractor for home repairs, you might say, "If we agree to do both the kitchen and the bathroom, can you lower the total cost by 10%?"

Using these strategies often results in more constructive conversations, rather than confrontations.

13.5 Negotiating Big Purchases

Cars and Real Estate are two areas where negotiation can save you thousands of dollars:

- **Cars**: Dealers often have leeway to reduce the sale price or throw in extras like free oil changes. Research the car's market value using reputable sites. Decide on your target and maximum price before you visit a dealership. Be ready to walk away if they will not meet your reasonable offer.
- **Houses**: Real estate is a huge purchase, so you want to be thorough. Learn about local housing prices, compare properties, and see how long each has been on the market. If a house has been for sale for a while, the seller might be more willing to negotiate. You can also ask the seller to cover some closing costs or make repairs before finalizing the deal.

With big purchases, make sure you have the finances ready—like being pre-approved for a mortgage—so the seller knows you are a serious buyer. This adds weight to your negotiation.

13.6 Salary Negotiation and Work-Related Deals

Salary negotiation is another crucial area. Failing to negotiate your pay can result in missing out on thousands of dollars over your career. Common reasons people hesitate include being afraid of rejection or not wanting to appear greedy. However, most employers expect candidates to negotiate. Here are tips:

1. **Speak with Confidence**: If the employer offers you $50,000 but you believe the market rate for your skill is closer to $55,000, politely say something like, "Thank you for the offer. Based on my experience and market research, I was expecting around $55,000. Is there room to discuss this?"
2. **Highlight Your Value**: Remind them of what you bring to the company—your skills, your track record, and how you can help them succeed.
3. **Consider the Whole Package**: If the employer cannot meet the salary you want, explore bonuses, flexible hours, remote work options, or additional training opportunities.
4. **Get It in Writing**: Once you agree on terms, ask for a written offer or contract so there is no confusion later.

Even after you start a job, you can negotiate raises or promotions. If you have increased your responsibilities or achieved outstanding results, that is a great time to approach your boss for better pay or perks.

13.7 Everyday Negotiations: Bills and Subscriptions

Negotiation is not limited to big events. You can also **negotiate your monthly bills**, such as cable, internet, insurance, or phone plans. Often, companies have better deals for new customers, but they might extend them to existing customers if asked. Or you might find promotional rates if you sign a longer contract.

How to approach it: Call customer service and say, "I've been a loyal customer for X years. I am noticing better rates elsewhere. Can we find a way to lower my monthly cost?" Stay calm and polite. If the first representative is not helpful, politely ask to speak to a supervisor or call back later. Persistence can pay off.

13.8 Overcoming the Fear of Rejection

Fear of "no" stops many people from negotiating. Understand that "no" is just one possible outcome, and it is not a personal rejection. If someone declines your request, it simply means they cannot meet it. You can then decide if you want to accept their last offer or move on. In some cases, you might negotiate again or explore other options.

One way to overcome fear is to practice in low-stakes situations. For example, try asking for a small discount at a local market or a boutique. Even if you only get a dollar off, you build confidence. Over time, you will realize that the world does not end if someone says "no," and that is a powerful mindset shift.

13.9 Politeness and Respect

Sometimes people think negotiation must be adversarial. In truth, the best negotiators maintain a friendly tone. Being rude can make the other party defensive or unwilling to compromise. Acknowledge the other person's perspective. For instance, a car salesman also needs to make a living. A landlord also has bills to pay. By showing understanding, you keep the conversation cooperative rather than combative.

Good phrases to use might be:

- "I understand where you are coming from. Let's see if we can find a middle ground."
- "I appreciate your offer. Is there any flexibility here?"
- "I realize you have targets to meet, but I also need to ensure the price fits my budget."

13.10 When to Walk Away

A vital element of negotiation is knowing when a deal is not worth pursuing. If you cannot reach acceptable terms, be ready to walk away calmly. This is why having a "walk-away point" is crucial in your preparation. For example, if you told yourself you would not pay more than $10,000 for a used car and the seller insists on $11,500, it is usually better to walk away. Sometimes, the seller may call you back with a lower offer once they realize you are serious. Even if they do not, you avoid making a regretful purchase.

Walking away demonstrates confidence and prevents you from spending beyond your means. It also sets a standard for how you want to be treated. If a negotiation feels one-sided or unfair, you have every right to leave.

13.11 Creative Negotiations Beyond Price

Remember, not all negotiations revolve around money. You can negotiate for additional benefits, services, or even payment plans. For instance:

- **Rent**: If you love an apartment but the rent is slightly high, ask if the landlord could include utilities, a parking space, or allow you to paint and personalize the space.
- **Health Care**: If you receive a big medical bill, you can sometimes negotiate a payment plan or even a lower total cost if you pay promptly.
- **Large Purchases**: Buying furniture or home appliances? Ask for free delivery, installation, or an extended warranty.
- **Business Deals**: Freelancers may trade services with other professionals. For example, a web designer could create a site for a copywriter who, in turn, writes blog posts for the designer's business.

Thinking beyond the obvious—simply price—can open doors to deals that satisfy both parties.

13.12 Handling Negotiation with Friends or Family

Negotiating with friends or relatives can be tricky, especially around money matters. Maybe you want to buy a car from a cousin or rent a room from a friend. Transparency is key to avoid damaging the relationship. Put the details in writing so everyone knows the agreed-upon price, payment schedule, or responsibilities. If the price is not satisfactory, be honest but polite. Sometimes, it is best to pass on the deal to keep personal relationships smooth.

Remember, friendship is more important than a small financial gain, so approach these negotiations with extra care. Be fair, speak kindly, and if your friend or family member cannot meet you in the middle, respectfully decline and stay on good terms.

13.13 Negotiation in Different Cultures

If you travel or work internationally, you might see that negotiation styles vary by culture. In some places, haggling at markets is expected and can be a fun social interaction. In others, prices are generally fixed, and trying to bargain might be seen as unusual. If you are in a culture that embraces bargaining, do not be shy about it—but remember to follow local customs and remain respectful. If you are unsure, observe how locals behave or politely ask how pricing usually works.

13.14 Negotiation Mistakes to Avoid

Even skilled negotiators can slip up. Some common mistakes:

1. **Being Too Emotional**: Losing your temper or showing extreme frustration can ruin the conversation. Stay calm.
2. **Focusing Only on Your Needs**: Listen to the other side. Understanding their viewpoint can lead to a compromise that benefits everyone.
3. **Accepting the First Offer**: Often, the first offer is not the best. Politely push for a bit more (or less) depending on what you want.
4. **Not Doing Research**: If you have no idea about market prices, you risk overpaying or undervaluing yourself.
5. **Taking It Personally**: Rejection of your proposal is not a rejection of you as a person. It is simply business or a different viewpoint.

Recognizing these pitfalls helps you correct course when negotiating. Treat each conversation as a learning experience.

13.15 Real-Life Examples of Successful Negotiation

1. **Evelyn's Furniture Deal**: Evelyn found a sofa she loved for $1,200. After chatting with the store owner, she discovered they had older stock in the warehouse. She asked politely if there was any discount on that version, or if they could include free shipping. The owner offered free shipping and knocked $100 off the price. Evelyn saved $200 total.
2. **Lamar's Cable Bill**: Lamar saw a promotion online for a new cable package that was cheaper than his current one. He called his provider and explained he wanted to stay loyal but could not justify paying more than the promotional rate. After some back-and-forth, the representative matched the promotional price for one year, saving Lamar $25 a month.
3. **Keisha's Job Offer**: Keisha was offered $48,000 for a job, but her research showed similar roles paid closer to $52,000. She politely stated she was excited about the position, but based on her experience and market data, she requested $52,000. The hiring manager came back with $50,500 plus one extra vacation day. Keisha accepted and felt valued from day one.

In each case, negotiation was respectful, fact-based, and ended in a better deal for the negotiator.

13.16 Building Confidence Over Time

Negotiation skills grow with practice. Start small. Negotiate a flea-market purchase or ask for a better rate on a gym membership. As you gain confidence, you can move on to bigger stakes—like salary and large purchases. Keep track of your successes. Even minor wins can boost your morale and remind you that negotiation pays off.

Also, learn from failures. If you fail to get a discount or your request is declined, examine what happened. Did you ask at a bad time? Were you unprepared? Did you push too hard or not enough? Each scenario offers lessons for the next negotiation.

13.17 Negotiation for Services and Freelancers

If you run a small business or do freelance work, you may be on the other side of negotiations—deciding how much to charge your clients. Remember these points:

1. **Value Yourself**: Set your rates based on the quality of your work, your experience, and the industry standard. Do not instantly lower your fees out of fear.
2. **Offer Packages**: Instead of lowering your price, you could bundle multiple services for a slightly discounted rate. This way, the client feels they are getting more value without you devaluing your work.
3. **Know When to Say No**: Some clients may haggle aggressively or want a price too low for you to profit. It can be better to walk away than accept a deal that drains your energy and undercuts your value.

Remember, negotiation for freelancers is a two-way street. You want to please clients, but you also need a fair rate to sustain your business.

13.18 Negotiation in Groups or Teams

Sometimes you will not negotiate alone—you might be with a group of coworkers or family members, and you need to present a united front. In those cases:

- **Coordinate Before Negotiation**: Make sure everyone agrees on the desired outcome and walk-away point. Inconsistency within the group can weaken your position.
- **Designate a Spokesperson**: Let the person who is most knowledgeable or comfortable speak during the negotiation, while others back them up if needed.
- **Communicate Clearly**: Resist the urge to argue among yourselves in front of the other party. Resolve differences beforehand, so you present a clear and consistent stance.

This approach can be crucial in events like negotiating a group discount for a large wedding or a team raise for a department at work.

13.19 Keeping Records and Receipts

Whenever you negotiate a deal, especially if it is complex or involves multiple parts, **document the outcome**. For instance, if you negotiated a lower rent or an added benefit in your rental agreement, ask for a revised lease or an email confirming the new terms. If you negotiated a salary or job perks, request a written offer letter. Having it in writing prevents misunderstandings. This is also true for large purchases—keep receipts, warranties, and any written promises in case of disputes.

13.20 Final Tips and Encouragement

Negotiation might feel awkward at first, especially if you are not used to it. But the potential savings and benefits are huge. Even small discounts can add up over a lifetime of purchases. Also, keep in mind that negotiation is a skill that goes beyond money. Learning to express your needs clearly, listen actively, and find common ground can improve relationships in many areas of life.

Key takeaways:

- You have the right to ask for a better deal.
- Preparation is your friend—know the market, set your goals, and be ready to walk away.
- Politeness and respect go a long way.
- Negotiation is a conversation, not a battle.
- Practice builds confidence and skill over time.

13.21 Chapter Summary

1. **Negotiation Basics**: It is about finding fair outcomes, not just "winning."
2. **Preparation Matters**: Research the market, set targets, and know your walk-away point.
3. **Everyday Uses**: Negotiation applies to cars, houses, salaries, bills, and beyond.
4. **Respectful Approach**: Remain calm, polite, and ready to listen to the other side.
5. **Long-Term Gains**: Saving or earning a bit extra through negotiation compounds over time.

13.22 Conclusion

Negotiation is a skill that can significantly improve your financial life. Whether you are buying a car, discussing your salary, or seeking a discount on monthly bills, your ability to politely and confidently ask for better terms can save or earn you thousands of dollars over the years. Coupled with the other financial habits you have learned—like budgeting, saving, and investing—negotiation empowers you to stretch your money further and achieve your goals faster.

CHAPTER 14: PLANNING FOR RETIREMENT AND LONG-TERM SECURITY

14.1 Why Retirement Planning Matters

Retirement might feel distant, especially if you are early in your career or managing daily expenses. Yet, planning for your later years is one of the most important financial steps you can take. Retirement planning ensures that you have enough money to cover your living costs when you stop working—or at least reduce how many hours you work. It gives you peace of mind and the freedom to make choices later in life.

A successful retirement plan is not just about having a certain dollar amount in the bank. It is about covering future costs, protecting yourself from unexpected events, and maintaining a comfortable lifestyle. Depending on your goals, retirement may include traveling, spending time with family, pursuing hobbies, or even starting a small passion project or business. However you imagine your later years, having enough financial resources can make those dreams possible.

14.2 Understanding the Basics of Retirement Accounts

Different countries offer various types of retirement accounts, often with tax benefits to encourage people to save for their older years. Common examples (in certain regions) include:

1. **Employer-Sponsored Plans**: Some jobs provide retirement plans—like a 401(k) in the U.S.—where employees can contribute a portion of their paycheck before taxes, and employers may match a part of that contribution.
2. **Individual Retirement Accounts (IRAs)** or other personal retirement funds: These are accounts you set up yourself if your employer does not offer a plan or if you want to save more on top of your workplace plan. Contributions may be tax-deductible or grow tax-free depending on the account type.
3. **Pension Systems**: Some workplaces or governments have pension programs. You typically earn a pension by working a certain number of years, and then receive guaranteed payments during retirement. Fewer

private companies offer pensions these days, so you may need to rely on personal savings and other accounts.

The key advantage of these accounts is the tax benefit. You can lower your taxable income today (in the case of a pre-tax account) or avoid taxes on future gains (in the case of a tax-free growth account, like a Roth IRA in the U.S.). Check the rules in your country for specifics. The earlier you start contributing, the more time your money has to grow.

14.3 Determining How Much You Need

One of the biggest questions in retirement planning is: **How much do I need to save?** The answer varies widely depending on your lifestyle, goals, and location. A general guideline some experts suggest is aiming for enough to cover around 70-80% of your current income annually in retirement, though this can be higher or lower based on how you plan to live. For example, if you earn $50,000 a year, you might need around $35,000–$40,000 per year in retirement.

However, some people want a more luxurious retirement, traveling frequently, or living in an expensive area, so they aim higher. Others plan a simpler lifestyle and might manage with less. Additionally, you must consider factors like expected health care costs, whether you still have a mortgage, and if you anticipate receiving any government pension or Social Security-type benefits.

14.4 The Role of Compound Interest in Retirement Savings

As we discussed in an earlier chapter on compound interest, the money you save and invest can grow exponentially over time. This is especially powerful in retirement accounts where your investments might compound for decades. That is why starting early is so crucial. Even small, regular contributions in your 20s or 30s can result in significant balances by the time you reach your 60s. The longer you wait to start, the more aggressively you usually have to save to catch up.

For instance, a 25-year-old who saves $200 a month and earns an average annual return of 7% might have a substantial nest egg by 65. Meanwhile, a 35-year-old who starts with the same monthly amount must often double or triple that contribution to achieve a similar total by retirement.

14.5 Investment Choices for Retirement

Retirement accounts typically allow a variety of **investment options**:

1. **Stocks (Equities)**: These can offer higher growth but also come with higher volatility. Over a long timeline, stocks have historically delivered solid returns, making them popular for younger savers who can handle market ups and downs.
2. **Bonds (Fixed Income)**: Generally safer but with lower returns. Bonds can help balance a portfolio and reduce risk.
3. **Mutual Funds and ETFs**: These spread your money across multiple stocks or bonds, providing diversification in a single investment. Many people choose index funds that track broad markets for simplicity and low fees.
4. **Target-Date Funds**: These funds automatically adjust their investment mix as you approach retirement. Early on, they hold more stocks for growth, then gradually shift to more bonds for safety.
5. **Real Estate or Alternative Investments**: Some retirement accounts or personal savings might include real estate or other assets like commodities. These can offer additional diversification if managed responsibly.

Selecting the right mix depends on your risk tolerance, how many years you have until retirement, and your overall goals. Generally, younger people can take more risk (more stocks), while those near retirement might focus on preserving wealth (more bonds and stable assets).

14.6 Employer Matches and Free Money

If your workplace offers **employer matching**—like matching your 401(k) contributions up to a certain percentage—take advantage of it. This is essentially free money. For instance, if your employer matches 100% of your contributions up to 5% of your salary, and you earn $50,000 a year, contributing $2,500 from your paycheck gets you another $2,500 from your employer. That is a $5,000 total added to your retirement account. Over time, this match can dramatically boost your savings.

Never leave this match on the table if you can afford to contribute, because it is one of the best immediate returns on your money. If finances are tight, aim to at least contribute the minimum required to get the full employer match, then gradually increase your contributions as you can.

14.7 Avoiding Common Retirement Pitfalls

Some mistakes can derail your retirement plans:

1. **Not Starting Soon Enough**: Waiting too long means you lose precious years of compound growth.
2. **Withdrawing Early**: Taking money out of retirement accounts before the permitted age can trigger penalties and reduce your future nest egg.
3. **Not Diversifying**: Putting all your savings into one company's stock or a single sector can be risky. If that sector or stock crashes, you lose big. Spread out your investments.
4. **Ignoring Fees**: High expense ratios or management fees can eat into your returns over decades. Always pay attention to the cost of your funds or advisors.
5. **Failing to Adjust Over Time**: As you get older, you may want to shift to safer investments. Sticking to an overly aggressive portfolio near retirement can lead to large losses if the market dips.

By being aware of these traps, you can avoid major setbacks and keep your retirement plan on track.

14.8 Planning for Health Care in Retirement

Health care can become a significant expense as we age. Even if you feel healthy now, you must plan for potential medical bills and long-term care. Some considerations:

- **Health Savings Accounts (HSAs)**: If your country or employer offers these and you have a high-deductible health plan, you can put pre-tax money in an HSA. Funds grow tax-free and can be used for qualifying medical expenses anytime.
- **Insurance**: Research your options for health insurance after you leave full-time work. Some retirees opt for private coverage, while others rely on government-funded programs.

- **Long-Term Care Insurance**: This helps cover expenses if you need help with daily living tasks later in life (like nursing home care). The earlier you purchase such insurance, the cheaper it usually is.
- **Emergency Fund**: Even in retirement, having a liquid emergency fund is wise. You do not want to be forced to sell stocks at a bad time to cover unexpected medical bills.

14.9 Social Security or Government Benefits

In many countries, the government provides a form of pension or Social Security as a baseline retirement income. How you integrate this into your plan depends on various factors:

1. **Eligibility Age**: Benefits often start at a certain age, but you might receive a reduced amount if you claim them early. Waiting longer typically increases the monthly benefit, though personal circumstances—like health or financial needs—may influence when you claim.
2. **Projected Amount**: Check government websites or statements that estimate your future benefits based on your work history and earnings.
3. **Supplement, Not Substitute**: Government benefits may not be enough to fund your entire retirement lifestyle. That is why having personal savings and other investments is essential.

14.10 Consider Part-Time Work or an Encore Career

Retirement does not have to mean completely stopping work. Some people choose to work part-time, either for extra income or to stay active. Others start a small business, turn a hobby into a side income, or do consulting in their area of expertise. This "encore career" can reduce how much you need from your savings each year, allowing your nest egg to last longer. It can also give you purpose and structure.

Still, do not rely solely on the idea that you "will just keep working." Health or family issues might prevent that plan. Use part-time work as a bonus rather than your only strategy.

14.11 Adapting Your Plan Over Time

Retirement planning is not a "set it and forget it" process. Life changes—like marriage, kids, divorce, inheritance, or shifts in the economy—may affect how much you can save or how you invest. As you move through different stages of life:

1. **Review Your Goals**: If you once dreamed of traveling every year in retirement but now want to stay close to family, your financial targets may change.
2. **Adjust Contributions**: Try to increase your contributions when you get a raise, pay off debt, or reduce expenses.
3. **Check Asset Allocation**: Your mix of stocks, bonds, and other assets might need rebalancing as you age or if market conditions shift significantly.
4. **Stay Informed**: Keep up with any rule changes in retirement accounts, tax laws, or government benefits so you can adapt your approach accordingly.

14.12 Spousal and Family Retirement Planning

If you have a partner or spouse, retirement planning should be a joint effort. Even if only one person works outside the home, you can often contribute to a spousal retirement account. Discuss your goals: Do you both want to retire at the same time or different times? Where will you live? How will you handle health care or life insurance?

If you have children, you may also consider how—or if—you will help with their college education. Some parents prioritize saving for retirement over college funds, arguing that children can get loans for school, but you cannot borrow for retirement. There is no one-size-fits-all answer, but open communication helps avoid surprises later.

14.13 Inflation and the Cost of Living

Over decades, prices for goods and services typically rise—a process called **inflation**. What $1,000 buys today may cost $1,500 or $2,000 in the future. That is why retirement plans must consider inflation. Simply saving a fixed amount of cash under your mattress will lose buying power over time. Investing in assets that grow at or above the rate of inflation helps ensure your savings keep pace.

Adjust your financial goals to reflect future costs. If you estimate $2,000 a month will cover your retirement bills today, factor in inflation for what those bills might be in 20 years. Many financial calculators let you input an assumed inflation rate (like 2% or 3% per year).

14.14 Estate Planning and Wills

Long-term security also includes what happens to your assets after you pass away. Having a **will** or an estate plan ensures your money and property are distributed according to your wishes. Without proper documentation, local laws may dictate how your estate is divided, potentially causing delays or conflicts among family members. Basic estate planning steps include:

- **Creating a Will**: A legal document stating who inherits your assets and naming a guardian for any minor children if relevant.
- **Designating Beneficiaries**: Many retirement accounts let you name beneficiaries. Ensure these are up to date.
- **Power of Attorney and Health Care Directives**: Assign someone to handle your finances or health decisions if you become unable to do so yourself.

You can update your estate plan as life changes—like marriage, divorce, the birth of a child, or major changes in your financial situation. Consulting a legal professional helps ensure all documents comply with local laws.

14.15 Avoiding Scams and High-Risk Deals

Retirees or people approaching retirement sometimes become targets for scammers or overly risky investment salespeople. Watch for signs of fraud, such as promises of extremely high returns with no risk, pressure to invest quickly, or unclear business models. Always research thoroughly, read official documents, and if possible, seek a second opinion from a trusted financial advisor or knowledgeable friend. Do not invest your hard-earned retirement money on a whim or because of a flashy seminar.

14.16 Working with Financial Advisors

As your finances grow more complex, you might consider working with a **financial advisor**. Advisors can help with investment choices, tax-efficient strategies, insurance, and estate planning. However, do your homework:

- **Fee-Only vs. Commission-Based**: A fee-only advisor charges a set fee or a percentage of your assets under management, and does not earn commissions from selling financial products. Commission-based advisors might steer you toward products that earn them the highest commission.
- **Fiduciary Standard**: Try to find an advisor who must act in your best interest (fiduciary).
- **Ask Questions**: Do not be shy about asking how they get paid, their experience, and their approach to investing and risk.

If hiring an advisor is too expensive or if you prefer a do-it-yourself approach, you can learn a lot from books, reputable websites, or free community workshops. Just be careful with online "gurus" who promise quick riches.

14.17 Adjusting Your Lifestyle for Retirement

Planning for retirement may also include thinking about how your **lifestyle** will change. Some people downsize their home once kids move out, reducing mortgage payments, property taxes, and maintenance costs. Others move to areas with a lower cost of living or better health care facilities for seniors. Consider these transitions:

- **Housing**: Will you keep your current home, buy a smaller place, or even rent?
- **Location**: Do you need to be near family, or do you prefer a warmer climate?
- **Transportation**: Retirement might reduce or eliminate daily commuting, so you could drop from two cars to one, saving money on insurance and upkeep.
- **Daily Activities**: Hobbies, volunteer work, and social gatherings can shape your expenses in retirement. Plan for them in your budget.

Sometimes, adjusting your lifestyle early—like living below your means—can free up funds to supercharge your retirement savings.

14.18 Staying Motivated for the Long Haul

Retirement planning is a marathon, not a sprint. Maintaining motivation for decades can be challenging. Some tips:

1. **Visualize Your Future**: Picture what your ideal retirement looks like. This keeps you focused.
2. **Track Milestones**: Celebrate when your retirement account hits certain targets—like $10,000, then $50,000, $100,000, and so on.
3. **Automate Contributions**: If money is automatically deducted from your paycheck, you are less likely to skip saving.
4. **Stay Educated**: Keep learning about personal finance. Knowledge helps you make better decisions.
5. **Adjust Your Plan as Needed**: If life changes or markets shift, tweak your contributions or investments, but keep the end goal in sight.

14.19 Chapter Summary

1. **Retirement Basics**: It is about ensuring financial security when you stop working.
2. **Starting Early**: Compound interest works best over time, so begin saving and investing as soon as possible.
3. **Account Types**: Use employer-sponsored plans, individual accounts, and take advantage of any matching contributions.
4. **Investment Strategy**: Diversify with a mix of stocks, bonds, and other assets suited to your age and risk level.
5. **Be Flexible**: Revisit your plan, adapt to life's changes, and stay focused on the long haul.

14.20 Conclusion

Planning for retirement and long-term security involves consistent saving, smart investing, and adjusting to life's twists and turns. While it can feel daunting, each step—such as setting up an employer plan or automating contributions—brings you closer to a stable and comfortable future. By starting early, diversifying your investments, and regularly reviewing your goals, you can grow the financial freedom to spend your later years on what matters most to you, whether that is family, travel, hobbies, or simply peaceful relaxation.

CHAPTER 15: TEACHING MONEY HABITS TO CHILDREN

15.1 Why Teaching Money Habits to Children Matters

Children grow up watching the adults around them handle money—whether it is parents paying for groceries or teachers collecting lunch money. Even if we do not talk about it directly, kids pick up cues about the value of money and how it is managed. By teaching them good money habits early, we give them tools for a lifetime. They learn to make thoughtful financial decisions, respect the work behind each dollar, and avoid common pitfalls like overspending and debt.

Many adults say they wish they had learned more about money as kids. They only realized the importance of budgeting, saving, and credit scores once they started dealing with bills, loans, or unexpected expenses in their 20s or 30s. By starting young, we can help children form healthy habits and mindsets before they make big financial decisions—like paying for college, renting an apartment, or buying a car.

15.2 The Benefits of Teaching Kids About Money Early

When children understand basic money concepts, they gain:

1. **Confidence**: They are less likely to feel overwhelmed by financial situations, such as managing an allowance or thinking about future goals.
2. **Responsibility**: They see that money does not just appear; it must be earned, budgeted, saved, or spent wisely.
3. **Independence**: They learn to make choices—like whether to spend on candy now or save for a bigger toy later—giving them a sense of control.
4. **Better Habits for Adulthood**: Early lessons can reduce the chance of running into chronic debt or financial stress later on.

15.3 Setting an Example: Modeling Good Money Behavior

Children often learn by watching. If we, as adults, spend mindlessly, keep secrets about money, or argue about finances, kids notice. By contrast, showing healthy money management—talking about budgets, comparing prices, and saving up for goals—teaches them that money is a tool for planning, not just impulse spending.

One simple way to model good behavior is to discuss money openly in age-appropriate ways. For instance, if you are at the store with a child, you might say, "We have $50 to spend on groceries this trip. Let's see how we can use that wisely." They learn that you do not just throw items into the cart; you look at prices and total costs. Over time, these small moments add up to a powerful lesson.

15.4 Using Allowances and Chores as Teachable Moments

An **allowance** can be a practical tool to teach budgeting. By giving a child a set amount of money each week or month, you let them practice making decisions—like whether to spend on treats right away or save up for something bigger. It also helps them learn that money is finite. Once they spend their allowance, they have to wait until the next allowance or find ways to earn more.

Chores linked to small payments can help children connect effort with earnings. For example, a child might get a little bit of money for washing the car or raking leaves. This fosters the idea that work brings in money—money is not just handed out endlessly. However, be clear on which chores are paid tasks and which are basic household responsibilities they do for free as family members. This balance prevents kids from expecting money for every helpful action.

15.5 Teaching Basic Budgeting Skills

Even at a young age, children can grasp the idea of dividing money into categories, such as **spend**, **save**, and **give**. Some parents use three jars or envelopes:

- **Spend Jar**: This is for short-term fun. Kids can use it on small treats like candy or stickers.
- **Save Jar**: This is for bigger goals—perhaps a new game or bicycle. It teaches delayed gratification and planning.
- **Give Jar**: This is for charity or helping others. Even if it is just a small amount, it builds a habit of generosity.

As they get older, you can introduce the idea of a **budget**—listing money that comes in and money that goes out for different expenses. A teenager might start budgeting for clothes, phone bills, or weekend entertainment. The key is consistency: show them how to track what they spend and see if they stay within their plan.

15.6 Explaining Saving and Delayed Gratification

Children are naturally inclined to want things immediately. Teaching **delayed gratification** is a core life skill. You might say, "If you do not buy candy every day, you can save enough in a month to buy that special toy." Encourage them to watch their savings grow over time and celebrate their achievement when they finally reach the amount needed.

Stories or simple analogies help, too. For instance, you can compare saving money to planting seeds. If you plant a seed and wait, you eventually get a bigger plant that gives fruit many times. If you eat the seed right away (spend the money impulsively), you miss out on the future rewards.

15.7 Introducing the Concept of Earning Interest (For Older Kids)

As children progress into preteen or teen years, you can introduce more complex ideas like **interest**. If they have a savings account at a bank, show them how the bank pays them a small percentage just for keeping their money there. Or you can set up a "family bank" system where you promise to add, say, $1 for every $10 they save by the end of the month. This mimics the concept of interest, teaching kids that saving can generate extra money over time.

This lesson can branch into a basic explanation of **investing**—putting money into something that can grow, like a small stock, mutual fund, or even a simple bond. While full-blown investing might be too advanced for younger kids, understanding that money can "work for you" sets a strong foundation.

15.8 Teaching Children About Needs vs. Wants

Many children (and adults) struggle with distinguishing **needs** from **wants**. Needs are essential for living—food, shelter, basic clothing—while wants are extras that enhance life. Explaining this distinction helps kids prioritize. For example, if they have limited money, they should aim to cover or contribute to their "need" items first, then consider "wants." This perspective can reduce materialism and teach them gratitude.

A simple activity is to have them list items around the house or their personal belongings under "need" or "want." For example, "shoes for school" vs. "the latest designer sneakers." This exercise can spark conversations about living within means and avoiding overspending for appearances.

15.9 Using Everyday Situations as Lessons

Teaching kids about money does not have to be a formal sit-down session. Often, the best lessons arise naturally:

- **Grocery Shopping**: Ask them to compare prices. "This cereal is $2.50, and the other is $3.25. What are the differences, and is it worth paying more?"
- **Family Outings**: Before going to an amusement park, say, "We have $100 for the day. Let's budget for tickets, food, and maybe a souvenir. If we want something extra, what can we cut back on?"
- **Online Shopping**: Show them how you research prices or read reviews to ensure you are getting a good deal, not just the first item you see.

Involving children in real decisions fosters a hands-on understanding of how money works in daily life.

15.10 Encouraging Entrepreneurial Thinking

Some children might show an early knack for business. Maybe they want to sell lemonade, bake cookies for neighbors, or craft bracelets. Encouraging small **entrepreneurial** ventures can teach them:

1. **Cost vs. Revenue**: If they spend $5 on lemonade supplies, they need to make more than $5 from sales to earn a profit.
2. **Marketing**: Drawing signs, setting prices, politely talking to customers—these skills help them see how presentation and communication can affect sales.
3. **Teamwork**: If they partner with siblings or friends, they learn to split tasks and profits fairly.

These small experiences can spark creativity and show children that money can be earned through effort and innovation, not just a "gift" from parents.

15.11 Guiding Teens on Credit and Debt

By the teenage years, it is vital to explain **credit**—how borrowing works, and why interest rates matter. Many adults get into credit card trouble because they never learned the basics as teens. A simple explanation might be:

- **Credit Card**: A tool that allows you to borrow money for purchases, but if you do not pay the full amount each month, you owe extra interest.
- **Interest**: The fee charged for borrowing money. High interest can double or triple the cost of an item if not paid off quickly.
- **Responsible Use**: Credit can be useful (like for emergencies), but it must be managed carefully.

If you feel comfortable, you might add a teenager as an authorized user on a credit card with a very low limit, so they can see how statements and payments work. Just ensure they understand the consequences of overspending and that you maintain strict boundaries to avoid real financial harm.

15.12 Discussing Future Goals (College, Car, etc.)

Teens often have big dreams—like buying a car at 16 or heading off to college. Use these milestones to discuss the reality of costs:

1. **Car Ownership**: Go beyond the purchase price. Talk about insurance, gas, maintenance, and registration. If they want a car, ask them to plan how they will cover those ongoing expenses.
2. **College or Trade School**: Explain tuition, room and board, scholarships, student loans, and part-time jobs. Guide them to research different programs and costs. If your family can contribute, let them know how much, so they can plan realistically.
3. **Gap Year or Travel**: If they want to travel after high school, help them budget for flights, accommodation, and day-to-day expenses. This can motivate them to save early and perhaps take on side jobs.

By connecting money to their specific aspirations, teenagers see the direct link between current habits and future possibilities.

15.13 Balancing Generosity and Self-Care

We want kids to be kind and generous, but also financially wise. Teach them that giving to others—through donations or gifts—is wonderful, but it should not put them in financial jeopardy. For instance, a teen might want to spend all their savings on a big birthday present for a friend. You can applaud their generosity while gently pointing out they also need to keep some savings for personal needs. This teaches **balance**: caring for others while also respecting one's own financial health.

15.14 The Role of Schools in Financial Education

In some regions, schools have introduced personal finance classes or units covering budgeting, credit, and basic economics. However, not all schools do. Even if a school offers financial lessons, parents and caregivers remain influential. Encouraging children to apply what they learn at school in real-life scenarios—like balancing a mock budget or comparing loan rates—can reinforce the concepts. If a school lacks such programs, parents can advocate for more robust financial literacy education or supplement at home.

15.15 Avoiding Materialism and Promoting Gratitude

Children often see commercials or social media that suggest buying products leads to happiness. Combat this by emphasizing **experiences** over **things**. Discuss how some of the best memories come from time with family or friends, not the newest gadget. Encourage them to be grateful for what they already have, by reflecting on the blessings in their life. For instance, you might share how some people around the world struggle for basic needs.

When your child does want a new item, ask why. Is it because they truly need it, or because it is trendy among friends? This helps them become aware of advertising and peer pressure. Over time, they will learn to spend mindfully and appreciate the difference between short-lived impulses and long-term values.

15.16 Handling Mistakes and Letting Kids Learn

Sometimes a child will make a poor choice—like spending all their allowance on candy and then regretting it when they see a toy they want. While it is tempting to bail them out, letting them feel the consequence (no extra money until the next allowance) can be the best teacher. They discover that impulsive decisions limit future options.

Encourage them to reflect: "What would you do differently next time?" Turn mistakes into lessons rather than scolding them harshly. This approach builds problem-solving skills and resilience.

15.17 Technology and Money Apps for Kids

Modern tools can make learning about money more interactive. Some banks offer special kid-friendly accounts with parental oversight. There are also apps that simulate budgeting or track chores and payments. They can show a child's balance in real-time, let them set savings goals, and offer small rewards when they stick to a plan. While technology is not a substitute for real-life practice, it can complement hands-on lessons.

15.18 The Importance of Consistent Conversations

Teaching money habits is not a one-time lecture; it is an ongoing dialogue. Children's understanding evolves as they grow, so revisit topics like saving, investing, and budgeting at different ages with more complexity. Keep the conversation relaxed—maybe during a car ride or while planning a family outing. The more open you are to their questions, the more comfortable they will feel discussing finances.

15.19 Helping Kids Think About the Future

As children reach their later teen years, they start imagining adulthood—jobs, places to live, and major life choices. Encourage them to think financially: "If you want to be a veterinarian, how will you pay for college? What if you need to relocate for a job? What monthly bills will you have?" This forward-looking approach helps them see that today's actions—like saving money, keeping good grades for scholarships, or choosing part-time work—can pave the way for a smoother adult life.

You can also introduce basics of **retirement planning** in a simplified manner: "When you work, you put aside some money for the future so you can stop working one day." While retirement is far away for them, starting the conversation early demystifies the concept.

15.20 Chapter Summary

1. **Early Lessons, Lifelong Impact**: Teaching kids about money at a young age fosters confidence, responsibility, and better decisions as adults.
2. **Model Positive Behaviors**: Let children see you budgeting, saving, and comparing prices. They learn through your actions as much as your words.
3. **Allowances and Chores**: Linking money to effort teaches the value of work, while budgeting a small allowance cultivates decision-making.
4. **Saving, Spending, and Giving**: Dividing money into different "buckets" helps kids practice delayed gratification and generosity.
5. **Preparing Teens**: Explaining credit, debt, and future goals ensures they enter adulthood with essential financial knowledge.

15.21 Conclusion

Teaching money habits to children is one of the greatest gifts you can give them. By showing how to earn, save, spend wisely, and share with others, you lay a foundation for a stable and fulfilling life. These lessons do not have to be complicated—they can be woven into everyday activities and conversations. The reward is seeing young people grow into adults who handle money with confidence, avoid destructive debt, and pursue their dreams from a place of financial security.

CHAPTER 16: GIVING, GENEROSITY, AND THE IMPACT ON WEALTH

16.1 Introduction: The Value of Generosity

Money does not exist in a vacuum. How we earn, save, spend, and invest it also reflects who we are as people. Generosity—whether it is financial donations, volunteering time, or sharing resources—can profoundly shape our relationship with money. Contrary to the fear that giving diminishes our wealth, many find that regular, thoughtful giving leads to a greater sense of abundance, stronger communities, and even more opportunities.

Generosity shows that money is a tool for growth, not just personal gain. By extending help to others, we often expand our own networks, learn new perspectives, and stay grounded. In a sense, giving reminds us that wealth is about more than personal comfort; it is also about creating positive change in the lives around us. That, in turn, can bring a deep sense of fulfillment and purpose.

16.2 Shifting from Scarcity to Abundance Mindset

A **scarcity mindset** focuses on the fear of not having enough. People who live in scarcity often hold onto every dollar, worried that sharing or giving will leave them vulnerable. An **abundance mindset**, on the other hand, recognizes that resources can be replenished through effort, creativity, and community support. While it is wise to manage money responsibly, there is also a belief that giving to others can coexist with building personal wealth.

Embracing abundance does not mean being reckless. It means believing that we can invest in ourselves and others. When we see opportunities instead of limitations, we become more open to new ideas, collaborations, and solutions. Generosity often fits naturally into an abundance mindset because we trust we will be okay even after giving.

16.3 Forms of Giving: Money, Time, and Resources

Generosity can take many shapes:

1. **Financial Donations**: This includes giving to charities, community groups, or individuals in need. It can be a regular habit—like setting aside a percentage of income for philanthropy—or occasional support for a special cause.
2. **Volunteering**: Some people give time instead of (or in addition to) money. They volunteer at shelters, mentor youth, or organize community projects.
3. **Sharing Skills**: Offering free tutoring, consulting, or creative work can be a form of generosity. For instance, a graphic designer might help a non-profit design a logo.
4. **In-Kind Contributions**: Donating items—like clothing, food, or electronics—also counts. Some organizations rely on physical donations to support their mission.

No matter the form, the principle is the same: using what we have to benefit others. Each method can enrich our lives and the lives of those we help.

16.4 Setting Aside Money for Charity

Many financially successful people practice a principle sometimes called **"tithing"** or giving a fixed percentage of income to charitable causes. You might choose 5%, 10%, or another percentage. The idea is to treat giving as a non-negotiable part of your budget—much like rent or savings. By making it a habit, you do not wait until you "feel like it" or see what is left over. You give proactively, which can create a mindset of gratitude and commitment.

If you are new to regular charitable giving, start small. You might pledge 1% of your income to a local shelter or global organization you care about. As you grow more comfortable, you can increase the percentage. The key is consistency: giving becomes a habit that transforms your relationship with money.

16.5 The Emotional and Spiritual Benefits of Giving

People who give often report feelings of **fulfillment** and **joy**. Giving can reduce stress, promote a sense of purpose, and even strengthen relationships. Some argue it also improves mental health by shifting focus from our own problems to the needs of others.

From a spiritual viewpoint, many traditions emphasize generosity as a virtue. Whether you practice a particular faith or not, there is a universal principle that supporting others can enrich our inner lives. It aligns with the idea that we are interdependent—our well-being is connected to the well-being of those around us.

16.6 The Ripple Effect of Generosity

When we give, the impact often extends beyond the immediate recipient. For instance, helping one person afford a school program might lead them to future success, which could allow them to help others in turn. Or donating to a small local business during a crisis might keep them open, preserving jobs and community services.

This **ripple effect** means generosity can create lasting change. It also fosters a culture of kindness. When we see generosity in action, we might be inspired to do the same. Over time, communities grow stronger and more resilient because people look out for each other.

16.7 Does Giving Actually Improve Your Wealth?

There is a common saying: "You cannot out-give the universe." While it may sound mystical, many financially successful individuals notice that when they give responsibly, they also grow their networks, gain trust, and learn valuable lessons. Here are a few practical ways giving can indirectly enhance your finances:

1. **Networking**: Being generous within a community or professional circle can lead to new opportunities, referrals, and friendships.
2. **Skill-Building**: Volunteering can teach leadership, organization, or problem-solving skills that you might not develop otherwise—skills that can benefit your career or business.
3. **Positive Reputation**: A generous person or organization often earns goodwill and a strong reputation, which can open doors to partnerships and clients.
4. **Mindset Boost**: Giving fosters a sense of abundance and gratitude, reducing fear-based decisions. This mindset can lead to bolder, well-considered moves in business or investing.

Of course, giving is not a direct get-rich scheme. It is more of a long-term perspective: by contributing to the greater good, we often end up nurturing an environment that also supports our own success.

16.8 Balancing Giving with Personal Financial Goals

It is essential to balance generosity with wisdom. While extreme self-sacrifice can cause financial strain, moderate and consistent giving fits well with a stable budget. Think of it like this: you want to **give from a place of strength**, not weakness. If you deplete all your resources, you might become dependent on others, which is not sustainable.

To find the right balance:

1. **Set a Percentage**: Decide on a realistic amount to give—like 5%, 10%, or a fixed monthly sum—based on your budget.
2. **Prioritize Your Basics**: Ensure you can cover rent, bills, and essential savings.
3. **Allocate "Extra" Giving**: If you receive a bonus or windfall, consider donating a portion of that too.
4. **Evaluate Regularly**: As your financial situation changes, adjust your giving. If times are hard, you might reduce temporarily. If you get a raise, you might increase your donations.

This systematic approach prevents guilt or impulsiveness, making generosity a steady habit rather than a random act.

16.9 Corporate Giving and Social Responsibility

Businesses also practice generosity. They sponsor community events, donate a portion of sales to charities, or set up scholarship programs for local youth. This can be a win-win: the community benefits from the funding, and the company builds a positive brand image. For entrepreneurs, weaving giving into your business model can attract socially conscious customers and employees who value working with or buying from a company that cares.

16.10 Volunteering and the Gift of Time

Not all giving is monetary. Many organizations appreciate **time** as much as or more than money. Volunteering can involve:

- Tutoring children in reading or math
- Serving meals at a shelter
- Organizing donation drives for clothes or food
- Helping an elderly neighbor with errands or home repairs

Volunteering has its own rewards: you gain perspective on different life situations, build compassion, and sometimes learn new skills that can be transferred to your personal or professional life. If you have limited financial means, offering your time and talents can be just as impactful as making a donation.

16.11 Teaching Children About Generosity

As we discussed in the previous chapter about kids and money habits, **generosity** is a key lesson. Show them how to set aside a small portion of allowance or chore earnings for donations. Involve them when you contribute to a cause—like letting them pick out toys to donate during the holidays. This hands-on approach teaches empathy and the idea that money can do more than buy personal items; it can help others.

Encourage them to volunteer, maybe at a community event or fundraiser. When kids see the direct impact of their help—like animals cared for at a shelter or families receiving warm meals—they understand giving is not just a chore; it creates positive change. These experiences often stick with them into adulthood.

16.12 Avoiding "Handout" Mentality: Responsible Giving

A tricky aspect of generosity is avoiding the **"handout" mentality**, where giving creates dependence rather than empowerment. For example, consistently giving money to someone who refuses to seek employment or skill development might hinder their growth. Responsible giving can mean providing resources, education, or opportunities so others can eventually become self-sufficient. This approach is sometimes called the "teach a person to fish" principle.

Similarly, donating to charities with transparent outcomes and sustainable programs ensures your contribution leads to meaningful, lasting benefits. Look for organizations that promote education, job training, or community development alongside immediate relief efforts. This way, you help people build a better future, not just solve an immediate crisis over and over.

16.13 The Joy of Anonymous Giving

While public donations or big gestures can inspire others, there is also beauty in **anonymous giving**. Some individuals prefer to donate or help quietly, without fanfare. This kind of giving often comes with a unique joy: you know you have done something good, but you are not seeking recognition or praise. It can be a humbling practice that keeps the focus on the recipient's needs rather than the donor's reputation.

16.14 Tax Benefits and Incentives

In many countries, charitable donations can reduce your taxable income. This is not the main reason to give, but it is a nice side benefit that can allow you to direct money to causes you believe in instead of paying a larger tax bill. Be sure to keep receipts or confirmation letters from registered charities, as you will need these when filing tax returns. If your donations surpass certain thresholds, you might have to fill out extra forms, so staying organized is important.

16.15 Stories of Giving Impacting Wealth

1. **Maria's Restaurant**: Maria owned a small eatery and regularly donated leftover food to a nearby shelter. Over time, local media noticed her kindness and featured her in a human-interest story. This led more people to learn about her restaurant. Her sales increased, she was able to hire more staff, and she continued donating leftovers. Her generosity ended up benefiting her business in unexpected ways.
2. **Jon and the Community Center**: Jon was a freelancer in a tight-knit town. He volunteered weekly at the community center, teaching computer skills to kids. Some parents learned about his professional skills and started hiring him for graphic design work. Later, when he needed help organizing a public event, the same parents and community leaders stepped in. He says volunteering strengthened his local ties and boosted his freelance career.

In both cases, giving was not a calculated plan to make money, but a natural expression of caring. Nonetheless, it paid off in terms of connections, referrals, and goodwill—highlighting how generosity can create positive cycles.

16.16 The "Pay It Forward" Ethos

The phrase **"pay it forward"** captures the idea that when someone helps you, you do not necessarily pay them back but instead help someone else in the future. This expands the chain of kindness. For example, if a mentor guides you for free at a crucial point in your career, you might later mentor a younger professional. The original mentor does not gain directly, but the overall culture of support grows.

Financially, paying it forward can mean using some of your extra resources or knowledge to uplift the next generation or those in need. Over time, this approach can build a community where people are more willing to help each other without expecting an immediate return.

16.17 Combating Greed and Materialism

Modern society often glamorizes having more—bigger homes, fancier cars, and designer products. **Generosity** acts as a healthy counterbalance to materialism. When you give, you actively acknowledge that you have "enough" to share. This can break the cycle of always chasing more possessions. It also fosters gratitude for what you already have.

Greed can trap people in endless comparison. But generous individuals often find a deeper satisfaction that does not depend on beating someone else. Instead of focusing on "me and mine," they think about "us and ours." That shift can reduce anxiety and dissatisfaction, making life feel richer in non-material ways.

16.18 Planning Your Giving Strategy

Just like you plan your budget or investments, you can plan your **giving strategy**:

1. **Identify Causes That Matter to You**: Maybe you are passionate about education, healthcare, the environment, or animal welfare. Focusing on one or two areas can make your impact more tangible.

2. **Research Organizations**: Look for charities with transparent finances and clear missions. Sites that track charity efficiency can help you ensure your money is used effectively.
3. **Set Goals**: Decide how much you want to give monthly or yearly. If you prefer volunteering, set aside a certain number of hours.
4. **Monitor and Adjust**: Over time, see if you are satisfied with the impact. If not, you can switch organizations or increase/decrease your contributions.

A giving strategy keeps generosity from being random. You direct your resources where they can make a lasting difference, just as you do with your savings or investments.

16.19 Encouraging Generosity in Your Community

Generosity can be amplified when groups come together. Consider organizing:

- **Community Fundraisers**: Gather neighbors to support a local cause, like fixing a park or assisting a family who lost their home to fire.
- **Workplace Drives**: Encourage coworkers to donate food, clothes, or money, perhaps matching their contributions if you are a manager.
- **Family Traditions**: Have an annual "giving day" where each family member chooses a way to help. This instills the habit of generosity across generations.

When communities pool their efforts, they tackle bigger problems and create a supportive network. People feel safer, more connected, and proud of where they live.

16.20 Making Giving a Part of Your Legacy

We often talk about **legacy** in terms of inheritance or passing on assets to children. But generosity can be part of your legacy too. You might set up a scholarship fund, leave a portion of your estate to a favorite charity, or pass down a family tradition of volunteering. Such actions show future generations that wealth is not just about personal comfort; it is also about communal uplift.

Encourage children or grandchildren to get involved in your charitable endeavors. If you donate to an environmental organization, explain why it matters. Invite them to volunteer with you. Over time, they will see generosity as a natural aspect of their heritage.

16.21 Chapter Summary

1. **Generosity Broadens Perspective**: Money is not just for personal use but can fuel community growth and help people in need.
2. **Abundance Mindset**: Believing in a world of opportunity allows you to give without fear, knowing you can rebuild resources.
3. **Multiple Ways to Give**: It can be financial, time-based, or sharing skills and resources.
4. **Indirect Benefits**: Giving can improve your reputation, build networks, and even enhance your sense of fulfillment.
5. **Planning Your Giving**: Set clear goals, research causes, and integrate generosity into your overall financial plan.

16.22 Conclusion

Giving and generosity extend the impact of all the financial wisdom you have acquired. By allocating some of your resources—be it money, time, or expertise—to help others, you enrich not only their lives but your own. Far from diminishing your wealth, generosity often expands your perspective, networks, and opportunities in surprising ways. This chapter closes the loop on money habits, reminding us that true wealth is not solely measured by what we keep, but also by what we share.

CHAPTER 17: NAVIGATING TAXES AND LEGAL STRUCTURES

17.1 Why Taxes and Legal Structures Matter

Many people see taxes and legal matters as confusing or frustrating. However, understanding the basics is crucial for protecting and growing what you earn. Whether you have a simple paycheck or run a small business, taxes affect your income. The right legal structures can shield your personal assets and give you certain financial advantages.

If you ignore taxes or set up the wrong legal entity for a business, you could face penalties, pay more than necessary, or miss out on helpful benefits. Handling these issues does not have to be intimidating. With some knowledge and organization, you can manage your taxes effectively and choose legal structures that safeguard your finances and help you reach your goals.

17.2 Understanding the Basics of Income Tax

Income tax is charged on the money you earn, such as wages, salaries, business profits, or certain investments. Governments use tax revenue to fund public services—like roads, schools, and healthcare. While each country has its own system, the general idea is that you report your earnings, apply any allowances or credits, and pay a percentage of what remains. Common terms include:

1. **Gross Income**: The total money you earn before any deductions.
2. **Taxable Income**: Gross income minus deductions or certain expenses. This final figure is what the tax rate is applied to.
3. **Tax Credits**: These directly reduce the amount of tax you owe (different from deductions, which reduce taxable income). Credits are often granted for specific activities, like education expenses or caring for dependents.
4. **Tax Deductions**: These reduce your taxable income. They can be business expenses, charitable donations, or other qualifying costs.

By knowing which credits or deductions apply to you, you can avoid paying more tax than necessary. For instance, if you donate to a qualifying charity, part or all of that amount might reduce your taxable income.

17.3 Types of Taxes Beyond Income Tax

Income tax is just one piece. You might encounter other taxes, such as:

- **Sales Tax**: Charged on goods and services when you buy them.
- **Property Tax**: Paid by homeowners or landowners based on the value of their property.
- **Capital Gains Tax**: Applied when you sell an asset—like stocks or real estate—at a profit.
- **Inheritance or Estate Tax**: Sometimes charged on assets transferred after someone passes away.
- **Corporate Tax**: Businesses pay this on their profits, depending on their legal structure and where they operate.

Each tax has its own rules and rates. If you run a business, you might deal with multiple taxes—like sales tax for products sold, plus income tax on profits. Staying organized helps you remain compliant and avoid unpleasant surprises.

17.4 How Employment Status Affects Taxes

Your work arrangement can heavily influence your tax obligations:

1. **Employee**: If you work for a company, your employer usually withholds taxes from each paycheck and pays them to the government on your behalf. At the end of the year (or tax period), you file a return confirming you paid the correct amount.
2. **Self-Employed or Freelancer**: You typically receive income without taxes taken out, so you need to calculate and pay taxes yourself (often quarterly). You can deduct business-related costs—like supplies, travel, or home office expenses—reducing your taxable income.
3. **Business Owner (Entity)**: If you form a separate legal entity, like a corporation or limited liability company (LLC), the business may pay certain taxes directly. You might pay yourself a salary or receive distributions. Each setup has different rules.

Knowing which category you fall under is key. For example, if you regularly take freelance jobs on the side, you might be responsible for estimated tax payments beyond what your main employer withholds.

17.5 Choosing the Right Legal Structure for a Business

If you operate any kind of side hustle or full-scale business, legal structure matters:

1. **Sole Proprietorship**: The simplest form—no separate legal entity. You and the business are the same for tax and legal purposes. This is easy to set up but leaves you personally liable for business debts or lawsuits.
2. **Partnership**: Two or more people share ownership. Profits and losses pass to partners' personal tax returns, but each partner can be personally responsible for the business.
3. **Limited Liability Company (LLC)**: Creates a separate entity shielding personal assets from certain debts or lawsuits. Often taxed similarly to a sole proprietorship or partnership (unless you choose otherwise), but with legal protection.
4. **Corporation (Inc.)**: A more formal entity, treated as separate from its owners (shareholders). Corporations can offer strong liability protection but might face "double taxation" if profits are taxed at the corporate level and again when distributed as dividends. However, some types of corporations (like S corporations in the U.S.) avoid double taxation under certain conditions.
5. **Nonprofit**: Formed for charitable, educational, or similar purposes. Nonprofits might gain tax-exempt status, but must follow strict rules about where money goes.

Each structure carries different tax and legal outcomes. If you are unsure, consult with an accountant or attorney. Sometimes starting simple (like a sole proprietorship or LLC) is fine, then you can shift to a different form if your enterprise grows.

17.6 Filing Taxes and Record-Keeping

Accuracy in tax returns relies on solid **record-keeping**. Save receipts, invoices, bank statements, and other documents that confirm income and expenses. Organized records make filing easier and reduce errors. For example, if you claim a home office deduction, keep records of utility bills and the square footage of your workspace. If you claim travel costs, log the dates, purpose, and expenses for each trip.

When you file, be mindful of deadlines to avoid penalties. In many places, personal tax returns are due once a year (like April 15 in the U.S., though the date can vary). Self-employed individuals might have quarterly filing requirements. If you cannot pay on time, you may arrange a payment plan, but you will typically owe interest and possibly late fees. Being proactive ensures you stay in good standing with tax authorities.

17.7 Reducing Your Tax Burden Legally

Tax planning is about minimizing how much you pay—*legally*. You might do this by:

- **Maximizing Deductions**: If you are self-employed, list every valid business expense. For individuals, check if you can deduct certain medical expenses, mortgage interest, or education costs.
- **Using Tax-Advantaged Accounts**: Contribute to retirement plans like a 401(k) or similar. This can reduce your taxable income now (with the money taxed upon withdrawal in retirement, depending on account type). A Roth-type account might work in reverse: you pay taxes on contributions now, but not on qualified withdrawals later.
- **Taking Advantage of Credits**: Some credits exist for child care, energy-efficient home improvements, or higher education costs.
- **Choosing the Right Business Entity**: As mentioned, some structures may lead to lower overall taxes if chosen wisely.

While tax avoidance (paying fewer taxes through legal means) is acceptable, **tax evasion** (failing to pay or intentionally misreporting) is illegal. Knowing the difference keeps you safe.

17.8 Navigating International Taxes

If you live, work, or invest abroad, taxes get more complex. You might owe taxes in multiple countries. Many governments have agreements (tax treaties) to prevent double taxation, but you generally must still report foreign income to your home country. For example, a U.S. citizen working in Europe often files a U.S. return and potentially claims credits for foreign taxes paid. Tools like the **Foreign Earned Income Exclusion** (in the U.S.) can lower the taxable portion of overseas income, but it comes with detailed rules.

If you invest in foreign assets, such as properties or stocks, be aware of local property taxes, withholding taxes on dividends, and possible reporting requirements back home. Failing to declare foreign accounts or assets can lead to serious penalties. Seek specialized advice if you have significant international dealings.

17.9 Common Tax Mistakes to Avoid

Even small oversights can cost money:

1. **Mixing Personal and Business Funds**: Failing to keep separate bank accounts for business can cause confusion and lead to incorrect filings or missed deductions.
2. **Ignoring Estimated Tax Payments** (For Self-Employed): If you do not pay quarterly, you might face underpayment penalties at year's end.
3. **Forgetting Small Income Sources**: Side gigs, rental income, or freelance projects must be reported. Tax authorities can track such earnings.
4. **Not Keeping Receipts**: Claiming deductions without proper proof can be disallowed in an audit.
5. **Missing Deadlines**: Late filing or payment can result in penalty fees. Even filing an extension requires some payment estimate in many cases.

Staying organized and aware of deadlines helps you avoid these pitfalls.

17.10 Planning for Retirement Using Tax-Advantaged Accounts

In a previous chapter, we discussed retirement planning. From a tax viewpoint, these accounts are powerful tools:

- **Employer-Sponsored Plans (e.g., 401(k))**: Contributions are often tax-deferred. You do not pay income tax on the amount contributed until withdrawal. Some employers offer a match, which is essentially free money.
- **IRAs or Personal Retirement Plans**: Contributions can be tax-deductible (Traditional IRA) or withdrawn tax-free later (Roth IRA), depending on the rules.
- **Self-Employed Options**: If you work for yourself, you could use a **SEP IRA**, **SIMPLE IRA**, or a **solo 401(k)**. These allow higher contribution limits than a standard IRA, reducing taxable income more.

The money in these accounts typically grows tax-deferred or tax-free, so more of your gains can compound over time. Just note that early withdrawals often face penalties, so plan carefully.

17.11 Understanding Capital Gains and Losses

When you sell a property, stocks, or other assets for more than you paid, the profit is a **capital gain**. Many tax systems treat these gains differently:

- **Short-Term Capital Gains**: Assets held for a short period (like under a year) often get taxed at higher rates, similar to regular income.
- **Long-Term Capital Gains**: Holding assets longer—over a year in many places—may qualify you for a lower tax rate. This rewards long-term investing over quick trades.

If you sell an asset at a loss, you might use that **capital loss** to offset gains, reducing your overall tax. Some rules limit how much you can offset in a given year, but you can often carry unused losses into future years. This strategy is called **tax-loss harvesting**.

17.12 Legal Structures for Real Estate and Other Investments

People who own rental properties or manage multiple investments might use an LLC or another entity for added protection. For example:

- **Real Estate LLC**: If you place a rental property in an LLC, only the LLC's assets are at risk if someone sues, not your personal savings or home. You then report rental income and expenses accordingly.
- **Holding Companies**: Some investors create a holding company that owns shares in various businesses or properties, consolidating control and possibly simplifying taxes.

These approaches can be complex. Always weigh the costs of forming and maintaining entities—like registration fees and annual reports—against the benefits of liability protection and potential tax advantages.

17.13 Handling Inheritances and Gifts

Wealth transfer can bring extra tax considerations:

1. **Estate and Inheritance Taxes**: Some governments tax the estate before assets pass to heirs, or impose a tax on the recipient. Exemptions often apply up to certain thresholds.
2. **Gifting**: Giving money or assets to relatives or friends might trigger gift taxes if the amount exceeds certain annual or lifetime limits.
3. **Step-Up in Basis**: In some places, inherited assets receive a "step-up" in cost basis, meaning capital gains are calculated from the value at the time of inheritance, not the original purchase price. This can lower taxes if heirs sell the asset later.

Planning with wills, trusts, or other estate tools can minimize confusion and taxes for your heirs.

17.14 Working with Tax Professionals

Sometimes it is worth hiring a **tax professional**—like a certified accountant or tax attorney—especially if your situation is complicated. They can:

- Find deductions or credits you might overlook.
- Guide you on entity selection and legal structures.
- Represent you in case of audits or disputes.
- Help you strategize for future years, not just file past paperwork.

When choosing a professional, look for relevant experience in your area (such as small business taxes, international issues, or real estate). Ask about fees upfront. Good record-keeping on your end will save their time and reduce costs.

17.15 Avoiding Tax Scams

Unfortunately, scammers try to exploit the complexity of taxes:

- **Phishing Emails**: Fraudsters pretend to be the tax office, asking for personal info. Official agencies usually do not request sensitive data via email.
- **Fake Calls**: Someone calls claiming you owe money immediately or face arrest. Real tax agencies typically send letters first and follow a formal process.
- **Tax Shelters**: Some promoters sell schemes claiming to "eliminate taxes" through fake deductions or offshore arrangements. If it sounds too good

to be true, it likely is. You, not the promoter, might end up in legal trouble.

Always verify communications directly with official tax websites or phone numbers. Do not click suspicious links or give private details to unknown callers.

17.16 International Business Structures and Offshore Entities

Larger businesses or online entrepreneurs sometimes consider forming companies in other countries with lower taxes. While this can be legal, it is heavily regulated. You must declare offshore income and comply with reporting laws—like the **Foreign Account Tax Compliance Act (FATCA)** in the U.S. or equivalent programs in other nations. Improper use of offshore entities can lead to accusations of money laundering or tax evasion.

If you genuinely operate in multiple countries, consult experts to structure your business fairly and comply with each jurisdiction's rules. The costs and paperwork might only be worthwhile at higher income levels.

17.17 The Importance of Contracts and Agreements

Taxes are only one side of legal security. Another is **contracts**:

- **Employment Contracts**: These define salary, benefits, and job responsibilities.
- **Rental Agreements**: Clearly outlines what the landlord and tenant must do—rent amount, maintenance responsibilities, and more.
- **Service Contracts**: If you freelance or hire freelancers, define the scope of work, payment terms, and deadlines.
- **Partnership Agreements**: If you co-own a business, put roles, profit splits, and exit strategies on paper.

Well-written contracts reduce misunderstandings and protect everyone involved. If disagreements arise, you can refer to the terms agreed upon rather than relying on memory or verbal statements.

17.18 Planning for Major Life Events

Several life milestones can trigger tax or legal changes:

- **Marriage**: Filing jointly or separately may change tax brackets and deductions. You might also need to update beneficiary designations on retirement accounts or insurance policies.
- **Having Children**: Kids may qualify you for tax credits, but also increase costs. You might want a will to name guardians.
- **Divorce**: Division of assets and child support can alter your tax situation. Alimony or spousal support might be taxable or deductible, depending on where you live.
- **Starting or Closing a Business**: Shifts in income and expenses may require new filings or dissolve existing entities.
- **Retirement**: You might move into a new tax bracket if you switch from a salary to retirement account withdrawals.

Staying informed helps you prepare for these transitions.

17.19 Keeping Up with Changing Laws

Tax laws and legal regulations evolve. Governments might modify rates, introduce new credits, or change the rules for business structures. Keep track of announcements or sign up for updates from reputable sources (like official government websites). If you have an accountant, they can inform you of major changes that affect your returns. Staying proactive can help you adjust your strategies promptly.

17.20 Case Studies: Simplifying a Complex Topic

1. **Nina's Freelance Expansion**: Nina started doing graphic design on the side while employed. At first, she just reported that freelance income as extra on her personal return. As her client list grew, she formed an LLC to protect her personal savings if a client sued or if she had issues with a contract. She meticulously tracked invoices and expenses, used a separate business bank account, and learned about quarterly tax payments. By the end of the year, she had reduced her taxable income with legitimate business deductions and gained peace of mind from the LLC's liability shield.
2. **Victor's Online Store**: Victor sold handmade goods online. He realized he had to collect sales tax from buyers in certain states. He researched each state's threshold for requiring sales tax collection (often called "economic nexus" rules). To simplify, he used an e-commerce platform that

automatically calculated and remitted sales tax in many areas. This diligence kept him compliant, avoiding fines or back taxes. Meanwhile, he also contributed extra to his personal retirement account, lowering his overall tax bill.

These examples show how knowledge of taxes and legal structures leads to a more secure and efficient financial life.

17.21 Chapter Summary

1. **Taxes Are Everywhere**: From income tax to sales tax, each affects your finances in different ways.
2. **Legal Structures Protect and Serve**: The right business form can limit liability and optimize tax responsibilities.
3. **Record-Keeping Is Essential**: Good documentation helps you claim deductions, file correctly, and stay safe in an audit.
4. **Plan, Do Not Evade**: Smart tax planning reduces your burden legally. Evading taxes risks penalties or worse.
5. **Seek Professional Help If Needed**: Complex situations may justify an accountant or attorney.

17.22 Conclusion

Navigating taxes and legal structures is part of being financially savvy. While it may seem overwhelming, the steps are simpler when approached methodically: keep detailed records, learn the rules for your situation, choose an appropriate business entity if needed, and stay updated on changes. With a bit of effort—or the help of a skilled professional—you can manage taxes in a way that protects your wealth and gives you confidence. By integrating wise tax and legal strategies into your broader money habits, you strengthen the foundation for all you have built so far.

CHAPTER 18: BALANCING HEALTH AND WEALTH

18.1 Introduction: Why Health and Wealth Go Hand in Hand

When discussing money habits, we often focus on saving, budgeting, and investing. But there is another vital element—your **health**. Physical, mental, and emotional well-being can greatly impact your financial life. Likewise, financial stress can harm your health if it leads to anxiety, neglect of self-care, or overwork.

Balancing health and wealth means recognizing that these two aspects of life support each other. Healthy individuals can often work more effectively, have fewer medical bills, and make clearer decisions. Meanwhile, a stable financial situation reduces stress and allows you to invest in things that keep you healthy—like quality food, fitness, and time for rest.

18.2 The True Cost of Poor Health

When you are in poor health, the costs can be staggering—medical bills, medications, missed work, or even the inability to work altogether. On top of that, stress from financial burdens can worsen health issues, creating a vicious cycle. For example:

1. **Chronic Illness**: Long-term conditions like diabetes or heart disease can lead to ongoing expenses for medication, frequent doctor visits, and potentially lower earning ability.
2. **Unexpected Accidents or Surgeries**: One accident can result in thousands of dollars in hospital bills if you lack insurance.
3. **Productivity Loss**: If you are always tired or in pain, you might not perform well at work, risking promotions or even job security.
4. **Emotional Toll**: Constant worry over health or financial problems can trigger anxiety or depression, which further impacts your life and finances.

Being proactive about health—through proper diet, exercise, and checkups—can reduce these risks and the associated costs.

18.3 Investing in Preventive Care

Preventive care means taking steps to stay healthy before problems arise. It might include:

- **Regular Checkups**: Catching conditions early often means simpler and cheaper treatments.
- **Vaccinations**: Prevent diseases that could cost you weeks of missed work and large medical bills.
- **Routine Screenings**: Tests for blood pressure, cholesterol, or cancer markers can stop small issues from becoming major.

Yes, appointments and screenings take time and sometimes money. However, preventing a disease or detecting it early often saves far more money (and suffering) than dealing with advanced illnesses. Some health insurance plans cover many preventive services, so check your policy and make good use of it.

18.4 Healthy Eating and Its Financial Benefits

Eating well can seem expensive if you think about fancy organic products. However, processed junk food, takeout, and sugary drinks can add up both financially and health-wise. By focusing on **balanced, home-cooked meals**, you may:

- Spend less money overall on food than if you eat out regularly.
- Reduce the risk of obesity, high blood pressure, and other conditions that lead to medical bills.
- Feel more energetic, improving productivity and reducing sick days.

Simple strategies include meal planning, buying in-season fruits and vegetables, and cooking in batches to save time. Learning basic cooking skills is an investment in your health—and it can be cheaper and healthier than relying on restaurants.

18.5 The Impact of Stress on Finances

Financial stress is a leading cause of anxiety and tension in many households. Worrying about bills, debt, or job security can trigger health issues like headaches, insomnia, or digestive problems. Chronic stress can also lead to unhealthy coping methods—like overspending on "retail therapy," smoking, or substance misuse—further harming health and finances.

Coping with stress proactively matters. Techniques like **mindfulness**, **regular exercise**, or **talking to a counselor** can ease mental pressure. In parallel, creating a clear financial plan—like a structured budget and debt repayment strategy—reduces the unknowns. This synergy tackles stress from both the mental and financial angles.

18.6 Work-Life Balance and the Value of Rest

Many people sacrifice sleep or personal time to pursue more income. While extra work can boost your earnings short-term, chronic overwork can erode your health. You might:

- Be too tired to exercise or cook healthy meals.
- Strain personal relationships, leading to emotional stress.
- Reach a point of burnout, affecting your performance and career longevity.

Conversely, a **work-life balance** allows you to recharge and maintain solid mental health. Taking days off, setting boundaries around work hours, and scheduling vacations or mini-breaks are not luxuries—they are investments in long-term productivity. Well-rested individuals often make better decisions and have fewer sick days.

18.7 Exercising Without Breaking the Bank

Gym memberships can be pricey, but you can stay active on a budget:

1. **Walking or Running**: Free, and you can do it almost anywhere.
2. **Home Workouts**: Many online videos offer routines that require little to no equipment.
3. **Community Spaces**: Parks, basketball courts, or school tracks might be open to the public.
4. **Workout Groups**: Local running clubs or sports meetups can provide motivation and social interaction at minimal cost.

Staying fit does not require an expensive fitness plan. The main challenge is consistency. If you find a routine you enjoy, you are more likely to stick with it, boosting your health and minimizing future medical expenses.

18.8 Health Insurance: Is It Worth It?

Health insurance (or similar healthcare coverage) can be a large expense, but the alternative—paying full price for major medical treatments—can be devastating. A single hospital stay for a serious condition can run tens of thousands of dollars. Insurance also often includes access to preventive services and checkups at lower out-of-pocket cost.

If your employer offers coverage, evaluate the plans carefully. If you are self-employed or between jobs, research what is available in your area. Look at the trade-off: monthly premiums versus potential medical bills. Even a high-deductible plan can limit your maximum out-of-pocket costs, providing a safety net against catastrophic medical events.

18.9 Dental and Vision Care

Oral and eye health are sometimes overlooked until problems arise. However, ignoring toothaches or vision issues can lead to bigger, more expensive procedures. Regular dental cleanings can detect cavities early, and routine eye exams can catch vision changes before they worsen.

These services can be pricey. Some companies offer separate dental and vision insurance, while others do not. You can also check local clinics, dental schools, or vision centers that provide reduced-cost services. Investing in regular checkups is cheaper in the long run than waiting for severe problems.

18.10 Mental Health and Its Financial Impact

Emotional well-being is part of overall health. Conditions like depression or anxiety do not only disrupt your daily life, they can also:

- Decrease work performance or lead to frequent absences.
- Increase healthcare costs for therapy or medication (if needed).
- Affect decision-making, possibly leading to risky financial moves or impulsive spending.

Seeking help—through counseling, support groups, or medication when appropriate—is a wise investment in your future. Many workplaces have employee assistance programs that offer therapy sessions at no or reduced cost. Good mental health fosters better relationships, sharper focus, and more stable money habits.

18.11 The Financial Benefits of Self-Care

Self-care includes anything that rejuvenates your mind and body—reading, meditation, hobbies, or just taking a break. While it might feel unproductive, self-care has real financial benefits:

- **Lower Stress**: Reduces the chance of stress-related illnesses, cutting medical bills.
- **Better Decision-Making**: A clear mind is less likely to fall for scams, overspend emotionally, or skip important financial tasks.
- **Sustained Energy**: You can handle work or side hustles more effectively, potentially increasing your income.

Incorporating daily or weekly "recharge" moments is not laziness—think of it as maintaining your most important asset: you.

18.12 Managing Time and Energy Wisely

Balancing health and wealth often comes down to **time management**. If you are juggling a full-time job, family, and a side business, you might neglect exercise or healthy cooking. Over time, that neglect can lead to more sick days and bigger medical bills. A well-planned schedule carves out space for both work and wellness.

For instance, you might:

- **Plan Meals and Grocery Trips**: A weekly schedule so you are not rushing for fast food.
- **Use Small Time Blocks for Exercise**: A 15-minute walk during lunch, short bodyweight workouts at home, or quick yoga sessions.
- **Set Sleep Times**: Aim for 7–8 hours a night, adjusting your bedtime and wake time consistently.
- **Prioritize Tasks**: Focus on the tasks that truly matter each day, both at work and in personal life.

When you actively plan your time, health does not fall through the cracks.

18.13 Workplace Health and Safety

If your job environment is physically demanding or has safety risks, ignoring those hazards can lead to injury and medical bills. In office settings, repetitive strain injuries (RSIs) or poor posture can also cause problems over time. Quick tips:

- **Follow Safety Protocols**: Use required protective gear, take scheduled breaks, and report unsafe conditions.
- **Maintain Good Ergonomics**: Adjust your chair, desk, and computer screen to avoid neck or back pain.
- **Speak Up**: If you notice a workplace issue, let your manager or HR department know. Preventing injuries is cheaper than dealing with them after they occur.

A safer work environment helps everyone, reducing absenteeism and improving morale.

18.14 Combining Fitness with Financial Savings

Sometimes you can merge physical activity with cost savings:

- **Bike or Walk to Work**: Saves on gas or transit fares, and keeps you active.
- **Grow a Garden**: Tending to vegetables or herbs provides exercise and yields fresh, low-cost produce.
- **DIY Home Maintenance**: Painting walls, doing yard work, or basic repairs can be a workout while saving money compared to hiring help.

Finding creative overlaps between fitness and frugality reinforces the connection between caring for your body and caring for your wallet.

18.15 Planning for Medical Emergencies (Emergency Funds)

We have discussed emergency funds as a buffer for financial surprises. Medical crises are a prime example. Even with insurance, you might face deductibles, co-pays, or out-of-network bills. Having a cushion helps you handle these sudden costs without going into debt. If you use your emergency fund for a hospital bill, aim to rebuild it once you recover. The unpredictability of health means repeated emergencies are possible, so staying prepared is wise.

18.16 Workplace Benefits: Using Them to Stay Healthy

Employers often provide benefits that can boost health:

- **Gym Membership Discounts**: Some companies partner with fitness centers to offer reduced rates or onsite facilities.
- **Wellness Programs**: Could include free health screenings, counseling hotlines, or stress management workshops.
- **Flexible Work Arrangements**: Telecommuting or adjustable hours can reduce stress, free up commute time for exercise, or let you manage medical appointments more easily.
- **Healthcare Flexible Spending Accounts (FSAs) or Health Savings Accounts (HSAs)**: Allow you to set aside pre-tax money for eligible medical expenses.

If your workplace offers these benefits, take advantage. They are part of your total compensation package and can save you money in the long run.

18.17 Overcoming Barriers to a Healthy Lifestyle

Common excuses for neglecting health include "I'm too busy," "It's too expensive," or "I don't know where to start." You can address these barriers by:

1. **Starting Small**: Instead of a full hour at the gym, try 10–15 minutes of stretching or walking daily. Progress gradually.
2. **Budget-Friendly Options**: Find free workouts online, join community sports leagues, or learn basic cooking to replace costly takeout.
3. **Education**: Read simple health tips, follow credible fitness influencers, or watch cooking demos. You do not need fancy courses to begin.
4. **Accountability**: Team up with a friend or relative who also wants to get healthier. Support each other with reminders and shared activities.

Small steps done consistently can yield big health improvements over time.

18.18 Mental Health Days and Burnout Prevention

Some workplaces allow **mental health days**—days off specifically to rest or address stress. Burnout arises when you push yourself too hard for too long, feeling emotionally and physically drained. Signs of burnout include constant exhaustion, cynicism toward work, and reduced performance. If you notice these, consider:

- Taking a break or vacation.
- Talking to a counselor or support group.
- Exploring if you can adjust your workload or schedule.
- Checking if your employer's health plan covers mental health sessions.

Preventing burnout safeguards both your health and career. Constantly working at half-energy due to stress can be less effective than a fully recharged approach.

18.19 Balancing Career Ambition with Personal Well-Being

Ambition can be great—it drives promotions, business growth, and higher incomes. The challenge is to temper that drive with self-care. If you let ambition overpower your health needs, you risk:

- Declining productivity and creativity over time.
- Potential serious illness or forced time off.
- Strained relationships, which can erode your support system.

Instead, set **sustainable goals**. For instance, if you want to expand your side hustle, build a plan that includes proper rest and exercise. Consider that an occasional "no" to an extra project might preserve your energy for better work on existing tasks. Remember, your aim is a long, balanced career, not short-term bursts followed by burnout.

18.20 Real-Life Examples of Health-Wealth Harmony

1. **Carlos's Wake-Up Call**: Carlos worked 60-hour weeks to increase his sales bonus but ignored routine checkups. After experiencing chest pains, he was diagnosed with high blood pressure. Realizing the financial risk of a major heart issue, he changed his schedule to fit in daily walks and better meal planning. Although he worked slightly fewer hours, his

productivity improved, and he actually earned more sales by being mentally sharper.
2. **Alana's Budget-Friendly Meal Prep**: Alana noticed she spent $300 a month on fast food and coffee. Beyond the expense, she felt sluggish. She started meal-prepping on Sundays and bringing lunches to work. She saved $150 a month and lost a few pounds. Her doctor visits went smoothly, and she rarely got sick. The money she saved went into a fitness fund for an occasional yoga class or healthier groceries.

Both examples highlight how small changes can reduce healthcare costs, increase savings, and enhance overall life satisfaction.

18.21 Chapter Summary

- **Health Influences Finances**: Poor health can lead to large medical bills and lost income. Good health supports long-term earning potential.
- **Preventive Measures Pay Off**: Regular checkups, healthy eating, and exercise reduce future expenses.
- **Stress and Overwork**: Chronic stress damages health and can drive poor money decisions. Work-life balance protects mind and body.
- **Insurance Matters**: Coverage can shield you from catastrophic costs.
- **Small Steps, Big Impacts**: Minor lifestyle tweaks (cooking at home, short workouts, mental health care) accumulate over time, saving money and improving well-being.

18.22 Conclusion

Balancing health and wealth is not about perfection—it is about making consistent choices that preserve your body, mind, and financial stability. By treating wellness as an investment rather than a chore, you reduce medical costs, stay more productive, and enjoy a better quality of life. As you continue on your financial journey, remember that you are your own greatest asset. Nourish yourself with healthy habits, manage stress responsibly, and make the most of benefits and resources around you. This synergy of health and wealth paves the way for a future where you have both financial security and the vitality to enjoy it.

CHAPTER 19: AVOIDING COMMON FINANCIAL MISTAKES

19.1 Introduction: Learning from Others' Errors

Throughout this book, you have learned a wide range of strategies—from saving and investing to managing taxes and caring for your health—all to improve your financial life. Yet even the most prepared individuals can stumble. Mistakes happen, and sometimes the best way to learn is by seeing what went wrong for others.

Avoiding common financial mistakes is about recognizing pitfalls before you fall into them. Often, these errors stem from emotional impulses, lack of planning, or unrealistic expectations. By understanding how mistakes develop, you can steer clear of them or correct course if you have already stumbled. This chapter breaks down common financial blunders and provides straightforward tips to stay on track.

19.2 Overspending: Living Beyond Your Means

One of the most widespread mistakes is spending more than you earn. This might happen gradually—small daily expenses that do not seem like much until you add them up. Or it may occur due to major purchases you cannot truly afford, like a car that strains your monthly budget.

Why It Happens:

- Temptation to "keep up" with friends or colleagues.
- Easy access to credit cards, encouraging impulse buys.
- Lack of real-time tracking, leading to surprise when bills come.

How to Avoid:

- Create and follow a realistic budget (see earlier chapters for budgeting fundamentals).
- Track expenses in a spreadsheet or app. Seeing the numbers in black and white can be a wake-up call.

- Build a "fun fund" so you have guilt-free money for occasional treats, instead of dipping into your main accounts.

Remember, living within your means does not imply no enjoyment. It just means planning your spending so you do not end up in a financial hole.

19.3 Ignoring an Emergency Fund

Life is unpredictable: jobs change, medical bills appear, cars break down. Without an emergency fund, you may reach for credit cards or loans to cover urgent costs, risking debt spirals.

Why It Happens:

- Underestimating the frequency or cost of unexpected bills.
- Impatience—preferring to spend surplus money on wants rather than saving.
- Lack of awareness about how small amounts can accumulate over time.

How to Avoid:

- Automate a portion of each paycheck (even $20) into a separate "emergency" savings account.
- Aim for three to six months of essential living expenses over time.
- Keep these funds accessible but not too convenient—like in a high-yield savings account.

Building an emergency fund may feel slow, but it provides immense security when crises strike.

19.4 Misusing Credit Cards

Credit cards can be helpful for building credit history, earning rewards, or managing cash flow. But they also pose a big risk if used carelessly. High-interest rates and easy swiping lead many into long-term debt.

Common Credit Card Pitfalls:

1. **Carrying a Balance**: Paying only the minimum accumulates large interest charges over time.

2. **Multiple Cards**: Juggling several high-limit cards can mask how much you truly owe.
3. **Cash Advances**: These often come with higher fees and interest rates than standard purchases.

How to Avoid:

- Treat your credit card like a debit card—only charge what you can pay in full each month.
- Check balances weekly (or more often) to prevent overspending.
- If you already have a high balance, focus on a debt repayment strategy (like snowball or avalanche methods discussed in earlier chapters).

A credit card used responsibly is an asset; used recklessly, it becomes a liability.

19.5 Falling for Get-Rich-Quick Schemes

Promises of fast wealth are tempting—multi-level marketing "opportunities," secret trading systems, or real estate programs guaranteeing million-dollar success in months. While some people earn money quickly, those cases are exceptions, not the norm. Most of these pitches are heavy on hype, light on real evidence.

Why It Happens:

- Desire for easy money or rapid results.
- Slick marketing that convinces you "time is running out" or you will "miss the boat."
- Lack of due diligence—people jump in without deeper research.

How to Avoid:

- Be skeptical of claims that sound too good to be true.
- Research thoroughly: read reviews, check legitimate business or consumer protection websites, and ask for verifiable case studies.
- Keep a long-term investing mindset. Real wealth typically grows over years, not weeks.

Patience, hard work, and proven methods usually yield better, more reliable outcomes.

19.6 Neglecting Insurance Needs

Insurance can feel like an annoying monthly cost—until you need it. Whether it is health, life, auto, or homeowner's insurance, coverage protects you from financial catastrophe.

Why It Happens:

- Hoping "nothing bad will happen to me."
- Trying to cut monthly expenses without evaluating long-term risk.
- Confusion over policy details, leading people to avoid choosing coverage.

How to Avoid:

- At minimum, ensure you have health insurance and auto coverage if you drive.
- If you have dependents, consider life insurance, especially term life, for a set duration (e.g., until kids reach adulthood).
- Shop around and compare quotes. One insurer's plan might be cheaper for you than others.

Better to pay smaller premiums consistently than to face massive bills after an accident or major medical event.

19.7 Missing Out on Employer Benefits

Many workplaces offer benefits that can save you thousands—like retirement plan matching, discounted insurance, or health spending accounts. Not using them leaves money on the table.

Why It Happens:

- Employees do not understand the plan details.
- Not reading the new-hire benefits booklet or ignoring HR emails.
- Assuming the sign-up process is too complex.

How to Avoid:

- Ask HR for a rundown of all benefits and deadlines to enroll.
- If there is a retirement match (like a 401(k) match in the U.S.), contribute at least enough to get the full match.

- Investigate any flexible spending or health savings accounts for tax advantages.

A few hours reviewing company perks can significantly boost your financial well-being.

19.8 Failing to Plan for Retirement Early

Retirement might seem far off, leading some to delay saving. But time is a powerful ally. Waiting even 5–10 years can mean you must invest far more to catch up.

Why It Happens:

- Focus on immediate bills or lifestyle, neglecting future needs.
- Belief that "I'll just work forever," which might not be realistic if health issues arise.
- Underestimating how much money retirement requires, especially with inflation.

How to Avoid:

- Start contributing to a retirement account as soon as you earn steady income.
- Utilize any tax-advantaged plans like a 401(k) or IRA if available.
- Gradually increase contributions when you get raises or reduce other expenses.

Let compound interest work in your favor by starting early, even if the initial amounts seem small.

19.9 Overly Concentrated Investments

Another common mistake is putting all your investment eggs in one basket—like a single company stock or one type of asset. If that sector tanks or the company fails, you lose heavily.

Why It Happens:

- Confidence in a hot stock or sector.

- Overestimating stability of an employer's stock (for employees receiving company shares).
- Lack of diversification knowledge.

How to Avoid:

- Spread out investments across multiple sectors and asset classes (e.g., stocks, bonds, perhaps real estate).
- Consider broad index funds that hold hundreds of companies.
- Rebalance occasionally, selling portions of what has grown too large to maintain a balanced portfolio.

Diversification reduces risk and evens out the impact of market volatility.

19.10 Overlooking Inflation and Opportunity Cost

Leaving large sums in a low-interest bank account for years might feel safe. But if the interest rate is below inflation, your purchasing power erodes over time.

Why It Happens:

- Fear of market fluctuations.
- Failing to compare interest rates or consider moderate, safe investments.
- Forgetting that 2–3% inflation over many years can seriously reduce real value.

How to Avoid:

- Keep only necessary short-term funds in cash for emergencies or upcoming expenses.
- Invest the remainder in vehicles that at least keep pace with inflation, like balanced mutual funds or higher-yield savings/bonds (depending on your risk tolerance).
- Regularly check if your money could be earning more elsewhere without taking on inappropriate risk.

Aim to preserve your wealth's real worth, not just its nominal figure.

19.11 Emotional Investing and Panic Selling

Financial markets fluctuate. Big downturns can spur fear-based decisions—like selling investments at their lowest point—locking in losses that could have been recovered over time.

Why It Happens:

- Emotional reactions to news headlines or market crashes.
- Lack of a long-term plan, causing people to view dips as permanent catastrophes.
- Herd mentality, following what friends or media say instead of personal strategy.

How to Avoid:

- Have a clear investment time horizon—money needed soon should not be in volatile stocks.
- Diversify so that not all assets fall at once.
- Remember market history: downturns are normal, and historically, markets recover given enough time.
- If panic arises, consult a trusted financial advisor before acting.

Keeping a steady hand during turbulent times often yields better results than impulsive buy/sell decisions.

19.12 Skipping Professional Advice When Needed

While do-it-yourself approaches can work for simple finances, more complex situations—like multiple income streams, inheritance matters, or international investments—may demand professional insight. Attempting to handle advanced tax or legal setups alone can lead to mistakes, fines, or missed opportunities.

Why It Happens:

- Trying to save on advisor or lawyer fees.
- Misjudging the complexity of personal circumstances.
- Preferring privacy or believing online research is enough.

How to Avoid:

- Seek a reputable accountant or financial planner if you have complicated earnings or major life changes.
- For big business deals or estate planning, consult an attorney.
- Ask about upfront fees or hourly rates to keep costs transparent.

The cost of a good professional is often lower than the cost of serious errors down the road.

19.13 Underinsuring or Overinsuring

We covered the risk of not having enough insurance. Conversely, overpaying for unnecessary coverage also wastes money. For instance, paying for special insurance riders you do not need or carrying high coverage for small possessions.

How to Avoid:

- Review policies yearly. Confirm your coverage still suits your life situation (car usage, home value, changes in family).
- Compare rates from different insurers to find the right balance of coverage and cost.
- Check deductibles. Sometimes a slightly higher deductible can drastically reduce premiums if you can cover that amount in an emergency fund.

Aim for an optimal level of protection—enough to safeguard you from big losses, but not so much that you drain resources on rarely needed extras.

19.14 Avoiding or Denying Debt Problems

Debt does not vanish if ignored. Late payments trigger higher interest rates, penalty fees, and credit damage. Some people feel so overwhelmed by debt they give up on budgeting or talking to creditors.

Why It Happens:

- Shame or embarrassment about large debts.
- Belief it is impossible to escape.
- Lack of knowledge about negotiating or consolidating options.

How to Avoid:

- Face the numbers: list all debts, interest rates, and minimum payments.
- Contact creditors to discuss possible lower rates, payment plans, or temporary hardship arrangements.
- Focus on the highest-interest debt first or use a debt snowball approach to tackle smaller balances for motivation.
- Seek reputable credit counseling if needed.

Honesty with yourself and active problem-solving can halt debt from spiraling.

19.15 Not Building Skills or Staying Employable

Your greatest wealth-building tool is often your ability to earn. Ignoring personal development—like failing to upgrade skills or adapt to new technology—may limit career growth or make you vulnerable to layoffs.

Why It Happens:

- Getting comfortable in one role, not wanting to leave comfort zone.
- Underestimating how fast industries change.
- Believing formal education ended after high school or college.

How to Avoid:

- Continuously learn: attend workshops, take online courses, read industry news.
- Network to keep up with job market trends.
- Pursue certifications or advanced degrees if they align with your career path.
- Seek challenges in your current job that expand your skill set.

Adaptable people are more likely to maintain or increase their income over time.

19.16 Failing to Teach Financial Skills to Family

If you manage all money matters alone without sharing knowledge or responsibilities, your partner or children may remain unprepared. Should something happen to you, they could be lost. Or they might develop poor habits that cause household conflicts.

Why It Happens:

- Belief that "money talk" is too complex or private.
- Cultural norms discouraging open discussions about finances.
- Time constraints or fear of letting family see potential mistakes.

How to Avoid:

- Involve your partner in budgeting discussions.
- Teach children basic money habits early (refer to Chapter 15 on teaching kids about finances).
- Keep a transparent record of bills, accounts, and passwords in a secure place so family members know how to access these if needed.

A family that understands and respects money fosters unity and resilience in tough times.

19.17 Trying to Time the Market

Some attempt to guess market highs and lows—pulling out money to "beat" a downturn or jumping in to catch the next upswing. This approach often underperforms a steady, long-term investing strategy.

Why It Happens:

- Overconfidence in ability to predict short-term fluctuations.
- Media hype around "imminent crashes" or "hot stocks."
- Lack of appreciation for how unpredictable markets can be.

How to Avoid:

- Practice dollar-cost averaging: invest a fixed amount regularly, regardless of market conditions.
- Keep an asset allocation that matches your risk tolerance and timeline, then rebalance periodically.
- Remind yourself that even professional fund managers struggle to out-guess the market consistently.

Time in the market often matters more than timing the market.

19.18 Neglecting to Update Estate Documents

Major life changes—marriage, divorce, birth of a child, relocation—can invalidate or complicate existing wills and beneficiary designations. If you fail to update documents, your assets might not go where you intend.

Why It Happens:

- Procrastination. Estate planning feels morbid or boring.
- Incorrect assumption that "my family knows my wishes."
- Unaware that some assets (like retirement accounts) pass via beneficiary forms, not wills.

How to Avoid:

- Review and update wills, living trusts, and beneficiary forms every few years or after big life events.
- Keep copies in a safe place and ensure close family or executor knows how to access them.
- Consult an estate attorney for more complex assets or family situations.

Proper estate planning spares loved ones from legal chaos and ensures your money supports who or what you care about.

19.19 Spending Money to Impress Others

Buying flashy clothes, new cars, or lavish vacations might temporarily boost your image, but if it leads to debt or minimal savings, it is not worth the façade.

Why It Happens:

- Pressure from social circles or social media, feeling the need to "show success."
- Lack of self-esteem, using material items to fill emotional gaps.
- Confusing wants with needs.

How to Avoid:

- Reflect on personal values—does that luxury watch align with them, or is it just to show off?

- Practice delayed gratification. Wait a week or month before big purchases to see if you truly want it.
- Set personal financial goals that matter more than fleeting approval from others.

True financial freedom often involves ignoring external judgments and focusing on your real needs and goals.

19.20 Ignoring the Importance of Health and Balance

As covered in Chapter 18, neglecting health—mental or physical—can result in higher medical costs, lower productivity, and damaged well-being. Overwork also risks burnout, undermining your ability to earn and enjoy life.

Why It Happens:

- Busy schedules or belief that health can be "dealt with later."
- Prioritizing immediate financial gains over self-care.
- Underestimating the long-term consequences of chronic stress.

How to Avoid:

- Schedule routine checkups and preventative measures.
- Budget for health insurance or wellness activities (gym, counseling, stress management).
- Set boundaries around work, ensuring adequate rest, exercise, and leisure.

A strong body and clear mind are invaluable assets on your financial journey.

19.21 How to Recover from Mistakes

No one is perfect. If you recognize that you have made one or more of these errors, do not panic. The steps to recovery typically involve:

1. **Honesty**: Acknowledge the situation. Face the numbers and facts.
2. **Education**: Learn or seek guidance from reliable sources.
3. **Plan Creation**: Map out how you will fix the issue, whether it is a budget revision, a debt payoff schedule, or professional help.

4. **Action**: Break your plan into doable steps. Consistency matters more than big, one-time efforts.
5. **Monitor Progress**: Check monthly or quarterly to see if you are improving. Adjust as needed.

You may feel discouraged, but mistakes are valuable lessons. Each error avoided or corrected strengthens your long-term financial stability.

19.22 Chapter Summary

- **Overspending** and lacking **an emergency fund** are key traps that lead to debt.
- **Misusing credit cards**, ignoring **insurance needs**, and missing **employer benefits** waste potential or create financial vulnerability.
- **Delaying retirement savings** or falling for **get-rich-quick schemes** hamper your future.
- **Concentrated investments**, **emotional investing**, and **market-timing attempts** often underperform basic, diversified strategies.
- **Skipping professional advice** for complex matters can be costly, as can **neglecting estate documents** and ignoring your **health**.

19.23 Conclusion

Every financial mistake has a root cause—be it ignorance, emotional impulse, or peer pressure. By knowing common pitfalls, you can catch warning signs early. Remember: success in money management is not about never slipping up; it is about minimizing the damage when you do and learning to do better next time.

CHAPTER 20: YOUR ONGOING JOURNEY TO FINANCIAL FREEDOM

20.1 Reflecting on the Road So Far

Over the past chapters, you have explored a broad spectrum of money habits: mastering mindset, saving consistently, budgeting, tackling debt, investing, negotiating better deals, planning for retirement, teaching children about finances, embracing generosity, handling taxes and legal structures, and caring for your health. Each piece of this puzzle contributes to the ultimate goal: **financial freedom**.

Financial freedom does not mean you must be a millionaire. It means having enough control over your finances so you can make choices that align with your values—whether that is spending more time with family, pursuing a dream project, or enjoying a comfortable retirement. As you reach each milestone, you gain confidence in your ability to handle money and shape your destiny.

20.2 Defining Your Next Goals

The journey does not end at a single goal. Perhaps you wanted to build an emergency fund, and now you have it. Great! What is next? Often, financial growth involves setting new, evolving targets:

1. **Increasing Investments**: Maybe you decide to raise your monthly retirement contributions or explore new investment assets.
2. **Paying Off a Major Debt**: Once you clear credit cards, you might target student loans or a mortgage.
3. **Starting or Expanding a Business**: If entrepreneurship appeals to you, your improved finances can fund a new venture.
4. **Achieving Work-Life Balance**: Perhaps you aim to reduce hours at your main job to focus on passion projects.

Align each new objective with your broader life vision. Money is the tool—your desires and values form the blueprint.

20.3 Embracing Continuous Learning

Finance is dynamic. Market conditions shift, tax laws change, new investing platforms emerge. Staying informed helps you adapt:

- **Read Books and Articles**: Keep refining your knowledge of personal finance topics.
- **Follow Credible Experts**: Online or offline, reputable financial educators can update you on fresh strategies.
- **Take Courses or Workshops**: Local community centers or online platforms often offer personal finance or investing seminars.
- **Learn From Others**: Join groups or forums where members share experiences and tips.

Continuous learning wards off complacency and ensures you spot new opportunities before they pass.

20.4 Periodic Reviews and Adjustments

Even the best plan needs updating. A helpful practice is scheduling **periodic financial checkups**:

1. **Monthly or Quarterly**: Review budget adherence, check saving rates, and track debt progress.
2. **Yearly**: Assess investments, see if you need to rebalance your portfolio, or if your insurance coverage is still appropriate.
3. **After Major Life Events**: Marriage, the birth of a child, moving, or job changes can alter financial needs significantly.

Look for areas to refine—maybe you can optimize certain expenses or shift money from low-yield accounts to better investments. Small improvements accumulate into big results over time.

20.5 Maintaining Discipline and Persistence

As we have discussed, financial success requires **discipline**—the ability to keep following your plan, even when distractions or temptations arise—and **persistence**—the determination to carry on in the face of setbacks. You might face:

- **Economic Downturns**: Market crashes can reduce your portfolio's value.
- **Personal Emergencies**: Medical issues, job loss, or family crises might force you to tap savings.
- **Temptation to Overspend**: Lifestyle inflation, peer pressure, or new gadgets can lure you off track.

Remember your "why." Whether it is providing a better future for your children or achieving personal freedom, that deeper purpose fuels the will to stay the course. Discipline and persistence, combined with well-structured plans, guide you through tough times.

20.6 Balancing Security with Growth

Over the course of your journey, you must balance the safety of your money and the potential for growth. Too conservative, and inflation erodes your savings. Too aggressive, and market volatility might keep you awake at night. A balanced approach:

- **Emergency Fund**: Always keep enough liquid assets for short-term security.
- **Core Investments**: Use stable, diversified funds or bonds to preserve principal value.
- **Growth-Oriented Investments**: Allocate a portion to equities or other assets that historically outpace inflation, depending on your risk tolerance and timeline.
- **Reevaluate**: As you age or if your goals change, adjust how much risk you can handle.

This balance shifts over time, but the core idea remains: protect what you have while seeking enough growth to meet future needs.

20.7 Staying True to Your Values

Money management is not just about spreadsheets—it is also moral and emotional. Align your financial choices with your values:

- **Ethical Investing**: If environmental or social issues matter to you, consider socially responsible funds or ESG (Environmental, Social, Governance) investments.

- **Responsible Spending**: Avoid companies you feel harm society or the environment, and support local or ethical businesses when possible.
- **Generosity and Community**: Continue practicing giving, volunteering, or mentorship. Sharing your success fosters a better world and nurtures a sense of fulfillment.

When your finances match your principles, you build not just wealth, but a life of integrity.

20.8 Teaching and Mentoring Others

If you have grown in financial literacy, you are in a unique position to help others. As we discussed in Chapter 15, you can teach children at home. But what about friends, siblings, or coworkers?

- **Share Knowledge**: Offer simple budgeting tips or point them to helpful books (maybe even this one!).
- **Encourage Healthy Habits**: If you see someone struggling with debt, gently suggest resources or share your own story.
- **Community Workshops**: Some people set up free sessions at local libraries or community centers, covering basic money management.
- **Online Groups**: If you are active on social media or forums, you might post short explanations on topics like saving or investing to spark discussions.

Spreading knowledge is rewarding. It reinforces your learning, too, because teaching clarifies your own understanding.

20.9 Avoiding Complacency

Once you experience some financial success—like paying off a significant debt or building a robust portfolio—complacency can creep in. You might loosen your budget or think you no longer need to track expenses. While it is fine to enjoy the fruits of your labor, be careful not to slide back into old habits.

A balanced approach is to celebrate milestones but keep the structure intact. For instance, if you have cleared all high-interest debt, you might slightly increase your "fun" spending—but still maintain a budget and a strong saving rate. Remember, money habits are for life, not just until you reach a certain net worth.

20.10 Embracing New Opportunities

Financial freedom can open doors. You might have resources to invest in a startup, take a sabbatical to learn new skills, or relocate to a city offering better job prospects. By being open to these possibilities:

- **Career Shifts**: If your finances are stable, you can risk moving into a field you are passionate about.
- **Real Estate Ventures**: You could consider buying a rental property if the numbers make sense, generating passive income.
- **Further Education**: With funds set aside, you can afford advanced certifications or degrees that elevate your career.
- **Travel or Life Experiences**: If you have always dreamed of traveling the world, financial security enables you to plan extended trips without jeopardizing your savings.

Each opportunity should still align with your overall plans and risk tolerance, but do not shy away from exploring new horizons.

20.11 The Role of Community in Financial Growth

Money habits flourish when supported by community. Whether it is a spouse, a friend group, or an online forum, having people who understand your goals and encourage you can make a huge difference. They can:

- **Offer Accountability**: Ask how your saving challenge is going or check if you stuck to the monthly budget.
- **Share Resources**: Suggest new tools, apps, or strategies they found helpful.
- **Provide Perspective**: If you are anxious about a market drop, they might remind you of past recoveries or successes.
- **Celebrate Milestones**: Recognize your progress, motivating you to keep pushing.

Conversely, negative influences can undermine your progress, so be mindful of who you consistently share financial aspirations with.

20.12 Continual Self-Assessment

Beyond monthly budgets and annual portfolio reviews, regular self-assessment fosters growth. Consider journaling about your financial mindset:

- **Am I slipping into old spending habits?**
- **Do I feel satisfied with my financial progress, or is there a gap to address?**
- **How are money goals impacting my relationships and personal well-being?**
- **What skills or knowledge do I still need to improve?**

Such reflections keep you connected to your deeper motivations, ensuring that money remains a means to an enriched life, not an end in itself.

20.13 Celebrating Wins, Small and Large

It is essential to reward yourself for milestones. Whether it is paying off a credit card balance or reaching a certain savings goal, a controlled celebration keeps motivation high. Just ensure:

- The celebration cost fits your budget. Over-spending to celebrate paying off debt defeats the achievement's purpose.
- You truly mark the moment—recognize how far you have come and how your actions made it happen.
- You use each win as a springboard for the next goal, riding the positive momentum.

Regular acknowledgment of progress reinforces good habits and highlights the value of discipline.

20.14 Managing Doubt and Fear

Fear of the unknown—like market crashes, job automation, or personal emergencies—can breed anxiety. While caution is wise, paralyzing fear is harmful. Tools to manage it include:

- **Scenario Planning**: Ask "What if?" for possible futures and note how you would respond. This sense of readiness can ease anxiety.

- **Building Flexibility**: Keep a portion of cash easily accessible. Maintain diverse skills in case your job changes.
- **Staying Informed**: Understanding the economy, your industry trends, and your investments helps demystify them.
- **Positive Self-Talk**: Remind yourself of past wins. If you overcame challenges before, you can handle them again.

Fear often loses power when faced head-on with facts, strategies, and confidence in your abilities.

20.15 Grasping That Wealth Is Not Just Money

True wealth encompasses time, relationships, health, and purpose. Plenty of high-income individuals still feel unfulfilled if they sacrifice family or well-being in pursuit of money alone. Conversely, some with modest means live richly, leveraging wise money practices to spend their days in meaningful ways.

Reflect on what truly brings joy and fulfillment:

- **Quality Relationships**: Cultivate strong bonds with family and friends.
- **Meaningful Work**: Even if you do not earn the highest salary, a job that aligns with your passion can be rewarding.
- **Experiences Over Possessions**: Travel, adventures, or shared activities can outweigh material accumulation.
- **Contribution**: Many find deep satisfaction in giving back—whether by volunteering, mentoring, or philanthropy.

Financial freedom is the foundation that grants you the space and security to nurture these elements.

20.16 Avoiding the "Arrival" Fallacy

The "arrival fallacy" is the belief that achieving a specific financial milestone will instantly solve all problems and make you perpetually happy. In reality, personal growth is ongoing. Reaching a $100,000 savings target might be exhilarating, but life continues the next day, possibly bringing new goals or challenges.

Instead of pinning all happiness on one milestone, enjoy the process. The daily improvements—building your skill set, helping family, maintaining good health—are part of a fulfilling life. Celebrate each achievement, but do not assume you are done evolving.

20.17 Handling Major Transitions and Setbacks

Even with strong habits, you may face major hurdles:

- **Job Loss**: Lean on your emergency fund, update your resume, and network for new opportunities.
- **Divorce**: Seek legal and financial advice to fairly split assets and establish a new budget.
- **Serious Illness**: Use health insurance or community resources to manage medical bills; tap your support network.
- **Economic Downturn**: Reassess your spending, maintain long-term investment strategies if possible, and keep building skills.

Tough transitions test your preparedness. Rely on the foundation you have built—emergency savings, diversified assets, supportive relationships—and adapt your plan. Mistakes or losses do not define you; your response and resilience do.

20.18 Visualizing Your Future

A powerful exercise is to visualize your ideal future. Close your eyes and imagine:

- What does your daily routine look like?
- Where do you live?
- How do you spend your free time?
- Who benefits from your generosity or mentorship?
- What legacy or impact do you hope to leave?

Emotional clarity about your desired future keeps you motivated to maintain strong financial habits. Each small decision—like skipping an unnecessary expense or upping an investment contribution—becomes part of crafting that vision.

20.19 Knowing When to Enjoy Your Wealth

Frugality and discipline are crucial, but so is knowing when to savor your resources. Some people accumulate large sums yet remain fearful of spending any of it. You should aim for a healthy balance: preserve security but also allow for experiences or comforts that enhance your life. A practical approach:

- Identify "must have" amounts (like an emergency fund or monthly savings), then allocate leftover funds for fun or convenience.
- Use specific budgets or separate accounts for travel, hobbies, or family adventures, so you spend confidently without dipping into essential savings.
- Periodically reevaluate if you are being too strict. Life is short; responsibly enjoying your money is part of the reward for your efforts.

This balanced approach prevents regret about missed opportunities or experiences.

20.20 Giving Yourself Permission to Evolve

The person you are today might have different dreams than you did five or ten years ago. Financial freedom includes the freedom to shift paths. Perhaps you want to pivot careers, take time for volunteer work, or move to a different country. Being locked into a single plan can stifle growth.

By keeping your finances flexible—maintaining liquidity, updating skill sets, and building multiple income streams if possible—you can pivot without derailing your stability. Embrace the chance to grow and redefine success as you mature.

20.21 Chapter Summary

1. **Financial Freedom Is a Process**: It grows from consistent habits, not a one-time fix.
2. **Set New Goals**: Once you achieve one milestone, identify the next target to maintain momentum.
3. **Keep Learning and Adjusting**: Markets, tax laws, and personal priorities change—stay informed.
4. **Discipline and Persistence**: Essential to overcome setbacks and emotional temptations.
5. **Value Health, Relationships, and Purpose**: True wealth extends beyond money.

20.22 Conclusion: The Journey Continues

Your quest for better money habits is both a personal and lifelong journey. Each chapter in this book aimed to give you a toolkit: from forming a positive mindset, creating budgets, and learning to invest, to safeguarding your health and giving generously. By weaving these habits into your daily life, you set yourself on a path toward real financial freedom—a freedom measured not just by the size of your bank account, but by the richness of your experiences, relationships, and contributions.

Even if you have setbacks or discover new challenges down the line, recall the core principles:

- **Mindset Shapes Outcomes**: Believe in your capacity to learn and improve.
- **Habits Compound**: Tiny, repeated actions yield massive results over time.
- **Focus on Long-Term Security**: Vision and patience outlast get-rich-quick temptations.
- **Adapt and Thrive**: Stay flexible, update plans, and remain open to new knowledge.

Now, armed with these insights, you are ready to forge your own path, step by step, day by day. Keep refining, keep growing, and remember to enjoy the journey. Financial freedom is not a distant finish line—it is a way of life defined by conscious choices, resilience, and a willingness to evolve. Wishing you success, fulfillment, and the sense of empowerment that comes from mastering your money habits for a brighter, more purposeful future.

Thank You for Reading

You have now completed *The Money Habits Book*. From setting goals and budgeting all the way to retirement planning, giving, and nurturing your health, each piece contributes to a solid financial foundation. You have the knowledge to make wise choices, avoid common pitfalls, and craft a life that aligns with your deepest values. The next steps are yours to take—continue learning, adapting, and building the future you envision. Thank you for allowing these pages to guide you on your journey toward financial well-being.

www.ingramcontent.com/pod-product-compliance
Lightning Source LLC
LaVergne TN
LVHW012106070526
838202LV00056B/5639